STUDENTS:
WHO
CONNECTS
YOUR
DOTS?

Students: Who Connects Your Dots?: A Complete Course on Critical Thinking
Copyright © 2024 by Jill Fandrich, PharmD

Published in the United States of America

Library of Congress Control Number: 2024903922

ISBN   Paperback: 979-8-89091-495-8
ISBN   Hardback: 979-8-89091-496-5
ISBN   eBook: 979-8-89091-497-2

All rights reserved. No part of this publication may be reproduced, stored in a retrieval system or transmitted in any way by any means, electronic, mechanical, photocopy, recording or otherwise without the prior permission of the author except as provided by USA copyright law.

The opinions expressed by the author are not necessarily those of ReadersMagnet, LLC.

ReadersMagnet, LLC
10620 Treena Street, Suite 230 | San Diego, California, 92131 USA
1.619. 354. 2643 | www.readersmagnet.com

Book design copyright © 2024 by ReadersMagnet, LLC. All rights reserved.

Cover design by Ericka Obando
Interior design by Don De Guzman

CONTENTS

Introduction for Students: Who Connects Your Dots? vii

PART 1 xiii

Chapter 1:   What is Critical Thinking? 1
Chapter 2:   Who Connects Your Dots? 8
Chapter 3:   Who's Hyped? 26
Chapter 4:   How Do You Decide? 33
Chapter 5:   Healthy Relationships 44
Chapter 6:   Activities and Academics 56
Chapter 7:   Obedience to Authority 63
Chapter 8:   Social Media and Electronics 74
Chapter 9:   Peer Pressure 84
Chapter 10: Why Identify? 95
Chapter 11: Kindness 109

PART 2 115

Chapter 12: Maintaining Your Health 117
Chapter 13: Who's to Blame? 125
Chapter 14: How Do You Communicate? 136
Chapter 15: Volunteering and Serving Others 145
Chapter 16: Innate Spirituality 154
Chapter 17: Leadership Skills 163
Chapter 18: Finances 173
Chapter 19: College and Careers 183
Chapter 20: Why All the Propaganda? 189
Chapter 21: Why Censor? 204
Chapter 22: Why Cancel? 209
Chapter 23: Conclusion 213

STUDENTS:
WHO CONNECTS YOUR DOTS?

A Complete Course on Critical Thinking

JILL FANDRICH, PharmD

Introduction for *Students:* Who Connects Your Dots?

As a student, what is your process for making decisions? What challenges are you faced with? How is your thought process affected by your challenges? By what means do you interpret information? How do you digest the content or data you absorb from news sources or social media today? How do you evaluate the validity of the information? What about information presented online or in a book? How do you know if the information is really true? Do you allow biases to affect your decision-making processes? How are your "dots" connected? How do you reason between opposing sides? Are you affected by the thoughts or opinions of others? Do you allow yourself to be pressured? What do you know about critical thinking?

One day, I overheard a student being pressured to skip classes by a group of kids who appeared to be classmates. She initially said no, and while I could see she meant it with her eyes, her wavering voice drew her peers to haggle her into agreeing to go along with them anyway. I could see her stressed and even tearful look as she collected her books from a bench and tossed them in her backpack. Two other girls were approaching and called to her, reminding her of a study group they apparently were all going to attend. One of the girls even exclaimed, "But what about your scholarship?"

What could possibly cause a person with a diligent commitment to abandon that commitment under the pressure or influence of another person or group of people? How prevalent is peer pressure in your environment? What are the consequences of not giving in to peer pressure? What if this student let her no, be *no?* What could have led to a different decision? How can the influence of another so easily sway someone? How can you say what you mean and act upon it without considering the influence of another?

Another time, I observed a similar situation in which some students attempted to "convince" a boy to smoke a cigarette, which they were dangling in his face. He let out a snide sound, followed by the comment, *"Get real."* Then he turned around and confidently walked away.

There were two different choices and two different future consequences. What caused one student to waver and decide to abandon her studies and the other to remain immovable in his stance? How are these circumstances similar? How do they differ? Who made the better choice? What is your decision based on? What might the consequences be in each example? How do you think each person was affected by the decision made? Who was right? Now what?

It is first important to bring yourself to an awareness of what is happening around you. Take a step back to collect information and assess the situation. It is essential that you begin to think critically about what is occurring "out there" in society and around you. This should lead you to ask question after question, seeking honest, substantial answers. Realize that the only logical answer lies in the ability to think critically about everything of importance.

A lack of proper thinking has crept into classrooms and society in general. You probably have experienced some form of difficult decisions in your own life by now, which illuminates the need to examine a topic such as this. What if you were presented with a sensitive dilemma or a peer pressure situation? How would you *instinctively* respond? What if you were equipped with the right skills to logically think through different possible outcomes and the consequences of each, then consistently choose the option with the most favorable outcome? What if you could read educational content, listen to any news source or any story in general, hear what is being said without a preconceived bias, and consider the information without becoming emotionally charged or passionate about being right? Then, listen to an opposing view with the same unprejudiced stature before formulating an opinion or drawing a conclusion.

This book provides the tools and insight needed to significantly improve your ability to decipher content without emotion, discern truth from "nontruth" with confidence and conviction, and increase your ability to handle any situation or decision with a logically based, unprejudiced conclusion. Critical thinking is a means to expand the way you think, open your mind to new thoughts and perspectives, increase the probability of uncovering factual information, and reduce the volatile impact fed from biased or opinionated sources.

It is time to return to the basics of thought processing. The most challenging problem you face, quite possibly, is dealing with the people around you, whether it is within your academic setting, your neighborhood, clubs or activities, or even within your own home! There is always a need to develop sound reasoning, open-mindedness, and insight and become more intellectually engaged.

In preparation for writing this book, I studied students of all ages and the circumstances they encounter on a daily basis. I observed news sources, campus life, actions, and reactions. I read numerous articles and books and even attended an in-depth study regarding critical thinking, human behavior, and responses. I questioned rational people and not-so-sensical ones as well. With each topic, I visualized situations relevant to each one and how they could be applied to academic, formal, social, and personal settings. I also extrapolated key findings from my experience from both my professional career and personal encounters. I organized the information in such a way that would be applicable from a student's perspective. When applied, these skills and strategies will prove to be effective, insightful, and thought-altering.

Relationships are the most important things in your life. It is logical to focus a significant amount of time and energy on understanding the nature of people and how your actions, responses, and decisions affect them. While it may not be easy, it is important to display tolerance as you listen to opposing views and opinions and value each person even if you disagree with their content. Learn how not to be sensitized by a different perspective or even influenced if the content is against your moral compass or what you know to be right. Be firm in your independent stance and *resist conforming* to someone else's ideas or emotional responses. Just as important as it is to have finesse and charisma in your interactions, you must also display the qualities of compassion and tolerance in the responses and decisions you make as well.

This book is interactive and meant to educate, inform, and instruct. Within each chapter, you will be brought to an awareness of particular content. You will be challenged to actively participate as you gradually yet consistently develop critical thinking skills. Throughout this book, you will explore skills that will refine you as a logical thinker and decision-maker. You will gain admirable qualities that set you apart, illuminate your current skills, and allow you to justify a position as a rational thinker and wise decision-maker. Read or listen to each section slowly and deliberately yet with vigor and passion while underlining, highlighting, and jotting down notes about key points you want to incorporate into your thought processes to improve your skills. Answer all the questions presented and consider new questions that spawn from them. While it may not be applicable to try these suggestions in every interaction, read or listen repeatedly to each section in order to program the information into your mind so you can access these "files" when the opportunity presents itself. Return and refer to these pages frequently, and even visualize the suggestions playing out in your specific setting. Think about them often and imagine different outcomes each time.

Ask yourself:

> *How could I have applied critical thinking to my interactions today?*
> *What mistakes did I make?*
> *How can I do it differently next time?*
> *Where could I improve?*
> *What did I do right?*
> *What have I learned from this experience?*

Journal your results, whether they are "in progress" or are already successes. Be sure to enter the dates of each entry, and be specific regarding the interaction, what questions you asked, how you researched and collected data, and how you reached a logical decision. Include what you did or did not like about your interaction. For your convenience, there is a list of suggested critical thinking questions and an example journal section at the back of this book. Each may be replicated for your convenience. Review your journal weekly to monitor your progress, reveal how you are growing in the process, and form a lifelong habit of logical thinking and decision-making.

To understand the dire need to train your mind to think this way, you will also be introduced to definitions, descriptions, relevant topics, applicable books paralleling current circumstances, and much more! By internalizing this information, you are sure to "imprint" inclusive thinking and successful traits into your mind's programming. While this is an enormous undertaking, learning about and truly understanding each chapter will undoubtedly grow you as a responsible person, ensure your ability to use logic and wise thinking favorably and productively, and launch you into becoming a decisive leader. Embrace each chapter enthusiastically and study it extensively. Understand what it means, the intent of the content, thoughts, methods, and reasons from the lists provided. Take time to answer all of the critical thinking questions listed. Visualize your own scenario with each question. Follow up with the concluding "Reflect" points at the end of each chapter. Engage in discussions and share your thought processes. Spend time on each category and decipher how to incorporate this information into your academic, social, personal, and even professional life. You will begin to notice logical thinking being displayed more and more naturally in all of your interactions. Ask the same questions as previously mentioned, and journal how you turned emotionally charged information into a well-processed and logical decision or conclusion, all while maintaining personal and formal relationships. Take the bias, emotions, and unwarranted opinions out of the situation. And finally, after the last chapter has been processed, go back to the beginning for a refresher!

The method in which this book is structured allows for the application to extend into formal studies as a separate course. Start your own critical thinking study using this book as a guide. Utilize the Reflect questions within the group and even expand on the topics by adding additional questions. Create a course within your church or other social group you are a part of. Consider the many sources where critical thinking may initiate compelling and thought-provoking discussions.

These suggested methods will allow you to get the most out of this book. Whether you are part of a live student body, are an online student or in a homeschool setting, or wish to lead a group into innovative thinking, this book will masterfully remind you of the common sense, logic, open mind, confidence, and tolerance you should build into the very nature of your being as you intellectually engage in your thinking, and display throughout every interaction.

Let the process unfold!

PART 1

CHAPTER 1

What is Critical Thinking?

What *is* critical thinking? Critical thinking (CT) is the ability to observe and think about a situation and to see and evaluate the validity or reality of it based on your own research and analysis without outside influence or bias. *Critical thinking is the analysis of an issue or situation and the facts, data, or evidence related to it.*[1] You take time to see the essential truth involved based on data, logic, and common sense. You "challenge" what has been said or shown and consider multiple possible answers or alternatives. *The key is to ask questions wherever possible.*

Along with using it to evaluate situations and events for truthfulness, CT should also be used in your general decision-making process. Sometimes, these strategies overlap, and sometimes they stand alone. For example, maybe you are asked to lie or cheat for your best friend and need to make a quick decision versus evaluating the truthfulness of news presented by a station desiring to mold your beliefs. These situations are different, yet both benefit from the same use of the CT process.

Many choices and decisions are made throughout each day that will benefit from CT. Consider each choice and evaluate the pros and cons. Evaluate opposing sides and the potential consequence of each decision made. Fifteen CT questions have been identified to help in the *decision-making* process.

CT Questions for Decision-Making:

1. What is the situation?
2. Who is involved?
3. What are your options?
4. Who will be affected by your decision?
5. How will you or they be affected by your decision?
6. Could anyone get hurt in the process?
7. Will your decision be something you can be proud of?
8. How will the decision shape your reputation or future?
9. How will the decision grow you as a person?
10. What are the potential consequences for each decision option available?
11. What is the right thing to do?
12. What obstacles might be clouding your judgment?
13. What option will lead to the best possible outcome?
14. What decision will be best for your legacy?
15. How did you reach your final decision?

CT is to be performed objectively, without influence from personal feelings, opinions, or biases. The focus should be entirely based on *factual* information. Perhaps even discover new ways of thinking about things. You must be able to do this without bias or prejudice.

Many different questions can be asked when seeking to discover the truthfulness of a situation or event. *Where is the evidence of proof? What is the source of evidence? Who is involved? Are they reliable? Is a source of funding somehow involved? How can you verify credibility?* This field of practice requires tremendous brain power and the capacity to think critically. Use this ability to think with an open mind and consider the validity of the presented information.

CT is a skill that can be practiced and mastered; it allows you to make logical and informed decisions to the best of your abilities. There is no particular standard for how CT occurs, and there are numerous variations to choose from. However, six basic concepts are presented here to guide you to becoming an exceptional critical thinker.

Six basic CT concepts to evaluate situations and events for truthfulness:

1. *Identify the situation.* It is important to *identify what is occurring.* What is the situation or problem at hand, and the factors that may be influencing it? Gain clarity of the situation, including who and what may be influential. Ask questions such as, *"Who is doing what?" "What seems to be the reason for this happening?" "What are the end results, and how could they change?" "What are the circumstances surrounding the occurrence or event?" "Why is it necessary?" "How did this transpire?"* and *"What caused the occurrence?"*

2. *Research.* The next step is to undergo intensive and independent *research,* comparing statements or arguments about the issue of concern. Arguments are often persuasive and influential. Therefore, it is imperative that you perform your research *independently,* and the resources must be verified as factual, reliable, credible, and unbiased. Evaluate the research and resources.

    Are the claims that are made "sourced" or "unsourced"? If the claims do not have a specified source, or you discover they are seeking to "hide" the source, that is a red flag, leading to the question of *why.* Then, research this new question and add the data to the other collected information.

    It is also important to be aware that the presented information may not be as it "seems." For example, a study may claim to use a placebo *as* a control, yet if you dig deeper, you may find it was not a "neutral" control. Perhaps a previous version of the drug is used *as* the "placebo" rather than a *saline-neutral* control. Or a product may claim to fix all your skin or weight concerns. Or a company may present a get-rich-quick scheme they claim "really works."

Or maybe you found a used gaming computer online for sale for a price that is "too good to be true."

Dig as deeply as necessary to reveal as much pertinent information as possible. Be sure to research both sides of the occurrence or claim and especially read the fine print. Collect as much information as possible from opposing sides or specifically from the source making the offer.

3. *Identify biases.* Biases are sometimes difficult to uncover, yet this is a vital part of the CT process. The most skilled critical thinkers seek to master this difficult ability. Strong critical thinkers do their best to evaluate information *objectively* and view the claims or consequences from both sides of an argument, statement, or decision.

It is important to be able to wade through the white waters of biases that likely are included on *both sides.* While *identifying biases,* it is equally important to set aside your own personal biases to ensure your judgment does not become clouded. Try challenging yourself to debate one side of the argument, justifying it until you win the argument. Then, do the *same thing* for the opposing side of the argument. Work just as hard individually for each side as you attempt to justify each to a win. Or consider possible consequences of a decision to be made. What are the compromises in each situation? What have you learned from this exercise? Were you able to collect enough information to justify each side to a winning position? Learn to see things from different vantage points and be objective in doing so.

Analyze the evidence and verify that the sources are credible and reliable. Questions to ask when evaluating biases include, *"Whom does this benefit?" "Does the source of this information appear to have an agenda?" "Is the source overlooking, ignoring, censoring, or leaving out information that doesn't support its beliefs or claims?" "Is the source using unnecessary language to sway the audience's perception of a fact?" "Where do you identify biases?" "Is there funding involved, potentially causing a bias?"* and *"Is there any emotion or intimidation present in the content?"*

4. *Logical reasoning.* Next, using logical reasoning and drawing conclusions based on the sound evidence you gathered from credible sources is important. In order to master the skill of CT, it is important to be able to *infer* and create an *educated "guess"* based on your thorough research. You must extrapolate and discover potential outcomes based on the raw data collected. Perform as much research as possible from various trustworthy and reliable resources.

    Analyze and evaluate all the data using logic and common sense. Assess the information and draw *your own* conclusions. As not all inferences will be correct, it becomes crucial to consciously gather as much untainted information as possible before reaching this decision.

5. *Discern relevance.* It can also be challenging, yet it's important to *discern the relevance* of the information for your consideration and seek the most relevant data. There may be a multitude of data out there to sift through regarding the topic. You must decipher what is most pertinent to reaching your desired destination. What is your end goal? Determine precisely what it is you want to uncover or discover. Guard against any inclination to show bias. Remain impartial and open to considering all information, yet use *your own sound* judgment to sift through the collected research.

6. *Unbiased discovery.* Be open to *unbiased discovery* by asking open-ended questions. This allows all possibilities without prejudice. Unfiltered and unprompted information may be revealed by asking questions in this format. A free flow of information is encouraged, and there is a greater potential for productive and favorable information to be produced that may further guide your evaluation of data. Open-ended questions also encourage learning and an exchange of ideas. They allow you to probe deeper and are non-

restrictive in thought. They may even allow for innovative responses or answers that spawn from the exercise of thinking, unhindered by a smaller scope of questioning.

Why think critically?

There are many decisions you are faced with to answer every day. While not every question needs a precise and particularly calculated answer, many will benefit from running them through the process of CT. However, suppose you practice the skills of CT regularly. In that case, you will realize it is possible to utilize this process extensively. It becomes programmed into your mind and is part of an automatic response you instinctively emit. You will have formed a *habit* of making logical, favorable, and productive decisions. While not every issue may "need" this process, it certainly won't hurt anything!

> *Critical thinking is the ability to think independently and rationally and to understand the logical connections between ideas. It is a skill that is essential for success in the modern world.*
> —Unknown

> *Critical thinking is the key to better decisions on the basis of knowledge and understanding.*
> —Jill Fandrich

> *Critical thinking is the key to unlocking the truth in a world filled with misinformation and uncertainty.*
> —Jill Fandrich

 Reflect:

1. What is critical thinking? What is the process of CT?
2. What are the two primary uses for CT? How can each of the uses apply to your daily life?

STUDENTS: WHO CONNECTS YOUR DOTS?

3. Name and describe the six basic CT concepts.
4. Create or think of an actual scenario where CT can be used. What questions will you ask? Journal your results.
5. How can you benefit from CT in formulating decisions? How can you benefit from it in deciphering the truthfulness of information?
6. Think of a sensitive situation. Apply CT concepts. What have you discovered? Journal on your findings.
7. Refer to the CT questions in the back of this book. Apply them to daily situations.

CHAPTER 2

Who Connects Your Dots?

What is meant by the words *"who connects your dots?"* Quite simply, *who* is influencing your thoughts, actions, and responses? Who is your life's most influential "person" or "source" of information? Do you draw upon content projected from friends, major news outlets, social media, or the Internet without question? Or do you consider the source, where it came from, whether or not bias is involved, what and whom it represents, who is affected by it, and what potential consequences might result, then think for yourself?

There was a time when the media was "called out" and reprimanded if the stories they presented contained false implications to the slightest degree. Currently, however, there is no consequence for "misinformation." As a matter of fact, misinformation is now actually *approved and encouraged.* Yes, misinformation is now permitted in our media culture and has existed for some time. Most major news outlets are derived from the *same* common source, owned by the *same* company, and produce the *same* deceptive content, with the goal of infiltrating, manipulating, propagating, or even instilling people with tainted data based on "its agenda" of what it wants you to know, believe, think, and how to react.

Knowing this, it is important to bring yourself to an *awareness* of this very operation that is occurring. Begin to ask yourself questions. Who owns each of the news sources? What is their common link or links? Where is the source of information coming from? How might the message be skewed?

STUDENTS: WHO CONNECTS YOUR DOTS?

Understand that you were not actually on location to know if this event really occurred or if the words spoken are valid. You do not have any proof of the expressed content. Are you allowing *them* to "connect the dots" for you, and are you accepting what they say as true and accurate? Or will you listen with an open mind, consider the content and the source, view opposing stations or vantage points, and derive your own conclusion?

How can you find out more information to substantiate the provided subject matter? Is it possible that there might be other versions of the story? Or could the story have possibly been altered to fit a scenario? How can you incorporate this insight into your analysis when evaluating all of the information? It is now imperative to consider all of these things.

From the moment you were born, other people have been programming your mind with "their" opinions, viewpoints, processes, and slews of other information. Your parents or guardians who raised you have shared their version of information, which was embedded into your mind. You absorbed additional information from teachers, friends, television, newspapers, media, social media, the Internet, books, and hundreds of other sources.

Other than what you *personally* have experienced, all of this data input has been presented to you with little to no evidence of truth to support or substantiate it. How do you know whether or not this information is accurate? How often do you actually think for yourself without outside influence? Did you realize that other sources have preprogrammed the multitude of your thoughts? Does this come as a surprise to you? Or did you understand this concept already? Are your automatic responses to situations in line with what you believe in? Do you even know *what* you believe in? What are your thoughts about *reprogramming* your mind to agree with your values?

In what ways do you learn things? What various sources do you use? Do you listen to the "worldview" and conform to what "it" thinks, says, and concludes? Does "it" have your best interests at heart? Be particular about your sources of education, and discover *who* wrote the books, constructed the YouTube, or is teaching the course, and know *what* they stand for, and possibly, who is funding them. Is there a good intention or an ulterior motive? It is becoming increasingly transparent that certain major and influential universities have taken an obvious and distinctive *political* stance rather than providing unbiased, factual, historical, and educational content.

Find the basis for their viewpoint, how and why they select the particular content, and how their conclusions are derived. What do they desire to achieve? It has also become apparent that you have become the ultimate source and target for initiating change in this world. If society can program students with the thoughts and ideation they want to provoke, rather than relying on the teachings of home and family values, the culture will begin to be, in essence, "brainwashed" to think and respond in the same ways desired and designed by the society, or the controlling governing body. Without realizing it, your ability to think freely and undefiled is gradually being *compromised* and *suppressed* through various, and even intricate, modalities.

Can you see evidence of bias presented in the news? Observe several different and opposing stations. Take some time to analyze your own thoughts regarding the content, the approach, and the viewpoint. Then, compare and contrast the similarities and differences you discovered through your analysis. What have you noticed? What is your go-to news source? Are you able to *objectively* watch different sources and uncover dramatically different vantage points and opinions of the same story or event?

Take a step back and consider what you have revealed. Do any that you have observed present objective and factual reports from an unbiased perspective, intending to inform you of proven details while allowing you to come to *your own* conclusion? The point here is not to provoke you to pick one side over another and follow blindly but rather to consider *both* or *all* sides and realize how the intent is quite often to *manipulate* you into taking "a" side. You are an intelligent person with the ability to think for yourself. You were born with a moral code and have an innate sense of right and wrong.

Now more than ever in history, you are losing the freedom and individuality your ancestors fought hard to provide. While it appeared gradual and subtle for decades, it is now *blatantly* apparent and exponentially driven that your freedom is being reframed with manipulation, brainwashing, and herd mentality.

Ways your freedom is being snatched:

1. *Through news media outlets.* It is quite difficult to deny that nearly all news sources are biased in one way or another. Understand that each one has *its* own agenda. Consider what that agenda may be, and use your own moral code to interpret the content. Bias generally carries with it an intent to persuade, manipulate, deceive, or even brainwash—research whom they are funded. The media no longer follows a code of ethics in presenting true and unbiased facts. *Know this* as you read or listen to any news source's content. Ask yourself who is presenting this information.

   What seems to be the reason for this portrayal or vantage point? What is the desired end result of the story? How could this change? Who will benefit from this viewpoint? Does the source appear to have an agenda? Does it appear to be ignoring, overlooking, or leaving out information in an attempt to sway the viewers? Find a news source with an opposing view. Follow through the same questions and assessment without prejudice, also discovering who funds it. Is it censoring anyone with an opposing viewpoint?

   Evaluate the information objectively and draw your own conclusions. Make a conscious effort to gather as much information as possible before coming to a conclusion. What information is most important? Evaluate the information you collected. What do you think is going on?

2. *By removing your history.* History is what it is. What would the point be to ignore it and pretend it didn't happen? That will not change the fact that it actually *did* happen. It is important to know what happened in the past, no matter how painful or fascinating, and to see how much we have grown as a country, continent, and world.

You have the right and *privilege* of knowing the truth of your forefathers and how you have been shaped *because* of it. "Society" today is trying to erase the past and pretend it didn't happen, or worse yet, *conceal* the details from you, relinquishing it from your mind. It is important to think about this fact and ask yourself why they would want to erase the knowledge of authentic past events from your mind. Think deeply about this question. How would you benefit from having yet another thing hidden from your mind? How many "political" things are currently being hidden from you already? Are you willing to give up more of your privileged rights?

Who or what is the source instigating this movement? Who benefits from attempting to erase historical facts from your information base? What does it solve by pretending historical events did not happen? What seems to be the reason for erasing historical facts from your mind? What is the end result of burying this disclosure?

Does it change the fact that it really *did* happen? *Why* are they intent on doing this? Who appears to be funding the movement? What information can you gather to shed more light on this subject? Where can you find unbiased data to extrapolate and discover your own conclusion?

3. *Through educational content.* Education at all levels should be, and was, a means for filling your mind with facts and actual events. The initial purpose was to grow in knowledge and gain a deeper understanding of how things work or operate, why things function the way they do, what actually happened, etc. The intent, and therefore, the content, has changed from factual knowledge of your choosing to biased agendas of what "the system" wants you to believe.

Why has society taken God out of schools? Who does this benefit? What appears to be its agenda for removing Him from the public school system? What about the information it is presenting in general? Is it based on fact, or is it biased?

What might its agenda be? Who is behind curriculum changes in the educational system? Is there a common link? Why was there gradual and now progressive conformity in the chosen content? Who is funding it? What seems to be the reason for these changes? What appears to be the desired end result? What will this change? Is it overlooking, ignoring, or leaving out information that doesn't support its agenda? Why might this be? Is it using unnecessary language or bias to sway your perception of *its* ideas or beliefs?

What might the reasoning be for the efforts to influence you into accepting its biasing of what should be factual and educational information? Where can you find unbiased resources so you can evaluate this information? How will you determine which sources are reliable, credible, and unbiased? What do you think is going on? Evaluate the information you collect, and draw your own conclusion.

4. *Through mandates.* "Mandates" are orders put in place by the authority of the one in a position to do so. What mandates are currently in effect in society today? How about recently? Have you suddenly been "forced" to act, think, or respond in specific ways based on particular information presented to you? Who presented this information? Who is funding it? What is the information on which the mandate is based? What seems to be the reason for the mandate?

Has the information been presented in a way to "scare" you into doing something? Has there been action by intimidation? What appears to be the end or desired result of the mandate? Who does the mandate benefit?

Does the source of the mandate appear to have an agenda? Is the source of the mandate overlooking, ignoring, or leaving out information that doesn't support the claims? Is any unnecessary information or language being used to sway your perception of the topic? Is there any censorship or "shaming" if you do not conform and agree?

Does this mandate interfere with any of your freedoms? Where can you find unbiased research from an ethical and trusted source to help understand the mandate? How have others "gained" or profited from the mandate?

How will you verify the credibility of the research and the source? Once verified, infer and draw your own conclusions based on the information you gathered. Follow the true and *real* science, and extrapolate your own logical result. What have you discovered? Did you reach this decision without prejudice?

5. *Through the entertainment industry.* Entertainment used to be lighthearted and enlightening, with the supposed intention of providing a pleasurable experience and some needed relaxation. It was an opportunity to let your mind drift from your current world and slip into the make-believe events of someone or something else. Today, a deliberate political message is portrayed and embedded in nearly all forms of entertainment, including movies, television shows, music, art, and even the advertisements in between.

Subliminal messages are most likely "guaranteed" to be a part of the included exposure. Are you familiar with all the subliminal messages encapsulated throughout all forms of entertainment? Commercials and advertisements are all about propaganda. Their goal is to mesmerize and standardize *their* view and agenda and imprint it onto you, causing you to alter your reasoning and belief.

What do you really know about subliminal messages? Where are subliminal messages hidden? What is their intent? Who benefits from them? How can you find out more about them? Why are people trying to influence you to change to their way of thinking and "normalize" that which is not normal via commercials and entertainment content? In the entertainment realm, who is sending a political message? What seems to be the reason for this message? Does the message have a bias? What appears to be the desired end result? How could this affect you? To whom does this message benefit?

Does the source of the entertainment appear to have an agenda? Are there any common links? Is the source ignoring, overlooking, or leaving out information that doesn't support its beliefs? Is the source using provocative, manipulative, or other forms of biased language to sway the audience's perception?

Maintain your ability to think for yourself based on your own standards, and beware of any intent to influence you and your family. What information is being fed through all the electronic devices held so dearly? Who controls these devices? Are they secretly invasive in your home? What are these devices capable of?

Where can you find unbiased and accurate information regarding all of this? What sources will you use in your research? How will you verify their credibility? What information is most relevant? Objectively analyze and evaluate this information and draw your own unbiased conclusion. What do you think is going on?

6. *Through Big Pharma and medicine.* "Big Pharma" is a large conglomerate of drug companies, individual proprietors, and then some. It has become a *powerful* and controlling entity of its own and via the government. Do your own independent research to find out details about who, what, and why it is. The goal here is simply to bring awareness to this topic, not define the precise composition.

There was a time when virtually the only source of drug advertising consisted of "Drug Representatives" propagating their product, attempting to influence physicians and other medical personnel to have their items chosen for a preferred drug formulary. Nowadays, not only is drug advertising in every venue, it now contains an inflamed sociopolitical agenda.

In order to make a logical and informed decision regarding your choices and conclusions, ask yourself many fact-seeking questions. Who is propagating the particular drug, vaccine, or other mechanism? Who is funding the propagation? Who is funding the clinical trials or research? What are they proposing? What seems to be the reason for doing this? What appears to be the desired end result? How could this change things?

How can you verify safety and efficacy? Who would benefit from this product being chosen for use or consumption? Who would benefit from the sale of this product? How long has the product been on the market? How many years and what type of research was performed regarding the product? Did it go through all of the proper steps of research and studies? How will you verify this? Do they reveal what was used as a placebo—something "safety-neutral" such as saline—or was it a previous version of a vaccine or other drug, thereby *not* neutral? Do they even use a placebo? Are the studies randomized and double-blinded?

What is the premise of this product? Are there other products similar to it? What makes one better than the other? What other choices do you have?

Does the source of the product appear to have an agenda? Is the source using unnecessary verbiage with the intent of swaying the consumer's perception? How are medical staff being persuaded to utilize the product? Are there incentives for its usage? Are hospitals receiving "kickbacks" for certain drug use or even diagnoses? How can you find out this information? What reactions have occurred since the inception of the product?

Follow the money and discover who receives monetary benefits in the medical domain. The ability to infer is vital in order to draw logical conclusions based on your findings. Where can you find untainted information? How will you verify your resources? What information is relevant for

STUDENTS: WHO CONNECTS YOUR DOTS?

discovery in order to draw your own conclusions? Assess the information based on unbiased raw data and extrapolate potential outcomes. What do you think is going on?

7. *Social Media.* Social media has taken the world by storm. Few, if any, cultures are not impacted by this form of communication. A choice can be made whether to use this device positively or negatively, to affect, inform, influence, or even manipulate others. That is in the eye and decision of the beholder.

   Along with the favorable ability to connect with long-lost family, friends, or other people, social media has also become an unfortunate method of propagation and political influence. Who has devised the message? What seems to be the reason for the message? Is there a reason behind the timing of the message? What appears to be the desired end result of the message? How could this affect you? Who is mainly affected? To whom does this message benefit?

   Does the source of this message appear to have an agenda? Are there monetary rewards involved? Is the message's source overlooking, ignoring, or leaving out pertinent information that doesn't support its beliefs or claim? Is there censorship to anyone with an opposing view? Does the source use particular verbiage or language to influence the reader or listener? Is there emotion built into the message? Is there an intent to instill fear in the viewer?

   Attempt to gather information from opposing viewpoints. Do not allow your personal biases to cloud your judgment. How can you independently verify the information? Research the content and source, collecting as much raw data as possible. Use logic to evaluate the information. Identify evidence that forms your beliefs. Draw your own individual conclusion. What do you think is going on?

8. *Through church and "religion."* There is a distinct difference between your beliefs and a "religion." While a belief is a mental conviction of truth, and a church is a body of believers, a "religion" is a man-made title with rituals or "works" to be performed to gain approval.

    As mentioned previously, conduct your own research for detail and clarity. This section is meant to bring awareness to this particular topic regarding propaganda. Propaganda and false prophets have been slipping into the church for centuries. It continues today in even more significant and obvious ways, although some ways are even more devious. This brings about the absolute need to evaluate information and engage in the process of CT.

    Who is presenting the message? What seems to be the reason for the message? What is the desired end result of the message? Who is the message intended to glorify? How are you impacted by the message? In what ways are you impacted? Who benefits from the message?

    Is there a financial incentive behind the message? Does the source of the message appear to have an agenda? Is there any political funding involved? Is the source overlooking, ignoring, or leaving out information that doesn't support its beliefs or claims? Does the source use language to sway the parishioners' perception of the facts? What information is relevant to determine the answers? Where can you find unbiased information?

    Research this data from an unprejudiced perspective. Evaluate and analyze the information, and ask yourself again, *who* is the focus of the *glory* of the message? Formulate your own conclusions. What has the information led you to discover?

9. *Through politics.* Politics. Oh my, politics. What can be said about politics? Politics was intended to be "for the people." The people were to elect officials who promised to work

hard and *serve the people.* The *people* were supposed to be in control, not the government.

It couldn't be further from this concept now. The political arena has become the center of self-serving agendas and a hub of propaganda. Thank goodness this is not the case with every elected official. However, it is the majority.

That being said, it is important to do your own research and decide for yourself the meaning and intention of political actions and agendas. Who is doing a specific action? What are they doing? What seems to be the reason for this action? Who is funding them? Why is it happening now? What are the intended end results of the action? How could this affect you?

Who does this action benefit? Is there a monetary reward behind, or for, this action? Does the source of the action appear to have an agenda? Can you decipher what the agenda is? Is the source overlooking, ignoring, or leaving out information that doesn't support the beliefs or claims of the action? Is the source of the action using persuasive language to sway the people's perception of a fact?

Is there censorship involved if there is an opposing view? Is there an intent to instill fear or intimidation in people? Look at the opposing side of the source of action. Ask the same questions from an opposing perspective. Where do you find biases? What supports either view? How does this benefit either side?

Independently research and verify the information discovered. What sources will you use? How will you deem them reliable? What information is relevant for clarity? Evaluate the claims of opposing sides, keeping in mind potential biases. Allow yourself to see things from both perspectives. Draw a logical conclusion based on your findings. What did you discover? And always take advantage of your right and privilege to vote and make your opinion count.

10. *Through the legal/judicial system.* The legal system is completely tied to the political system, being a branch of it. Some officials of the court are elected, and some are not. The people elect some, and some are elected by the people who were elected. Your own research will provide more clarity to these words.

    It is important to ask the same questions regarding specifics in the legal system for the same reasons mentioned previously. Make yourself aware of potential bias and underlying reasons, such as financial, reputational, or even positional pressure. Always seek to find out who may be funding a person or event that may be occurring. Evaluate unbiased information you obtained through your own research. What do you conclude?

11. *Science and research.* Science *is* knowledge. It is a body of *facts* learned through study, observation, or experience. Generally, if you want to find the truth regarding something material or organic, you follow the science. *However,* even sources or the appearance of "science" can be fabricated or manipulated by a human hand. This again leads to the importance of the vital process of CT.

    Regarding a new "vaccine" or a suspicious virus, rather than make assumptions or engage in a "herd mentality," do your own research. Follow unbiased and untainted science. If someone or something is concealing evidence or will not reveal a source, it is important to ask yourself *why.* Who is making a scientific claim? What is the claim? What seems to be the reason for the claim? Are they offering full disclosure? What appears to be the end result of the claim? How could this affect you? How does this affect them?

    To whom does this claim benefit? *Follow the money.* Are there monetary benefits for this claim? Are there financial benefits based on a volume of people conceding to this claim? Does the source of the claim appear to have an agenda regarding it? Are there any other possible agendas involved? Is the source overlooking, ignoring, or leaving out information that doesn't support the claim?

Is there censorship occurring for anyone with an opposing view? Is any unnecessary or persuasive language used to sway the end user's perception of the claim? Is there intimidation involved in promoting the product? How about fear? Is there an intention meant to create fear in people?

Where can you find information about sources not biased toward this claim? Research many unbiased sources as you seek answers and factual knowledge. Observe information from opposing sides of the claim. Is the research itself credible? Evaluate each side without prejudice. Determine the relevance of the information and focus on what is most important regarding the claim. Verify that the sources are credible. How will you determine if they are credible?

Make sure you know who is funding the research you are examining. What would allow you to put something into your body without verifying facts regarding the ingredients? Know what goes into your body. Assess all of the information you gathered and analyze the data. Draw your own conclusion based on *your* research. Where does it take you? What conclusions do you arrive at?

12. *Through literature.* Literature can be entertaining, informative, educational, persuasive, humorous, sad, etc. It can be almost anything. Writing has been a part of society for countless generations as a way of communicating, educating, and preserving thoughts and ideas. Unfortunately, literature can also be deceptive.

Relating true, honest, accurate, and completely factual content is no longer required. So, once again, it is important to ask many questions and consider the research you have personally collected regarding the literature and the source. Who is the author? What did they write? What seems to be the reason for composing the material? What appears to be the desired result of the material? How could this affect you? How could it affect the author? Whom does it benefit?

Does the author appear to have an agenda? Are you able to identify a political agenda? Is the author overlooking, ignoring, or leaving out information that may be contrary to the intended claim? Does the author use persuasive language to sway the reader's perception? Is there strong emotion, or any emotion, tied to the material?

What can you learn about the opposing view if it poses an argument? How can you verify the facts or content within the material? Is it truthful? Is there some type of funding for the project? What unbiased sources can you use to find out more information? How will you verify the sources? Is the material meant for pleasure or to inform or persuade? Does the author reveal sources used for the material?

Collect as much information as possible from credible sources. Evaluate the information objectively and draw your own conclusion. What did you discover about the material? What about the author? What conclusion have you reached?

13. *Through family, friends, or associates.* People you associate with can be very influential for numerous reasons. Perhaps you are fond of them, loyal, curious, indebted, opposed, or maybe even intimidated by them. Knowing the motive behind what people do, say, or even why is not always easy.

    It is important to decipher the person's validity and any motives or intentions they may have, especially regarding you. Sometimes, there is controversy within your own family unit. Lately, it may even be derived from a politically different standpoint. Be able to identify the necessity to evaluate them as well. What are they doing, asking of you, or standing for? What seems to be the reason for this? What appears to be the desired end result? How would this affect you? How would it affect them?

    Who does this action or request benefit? Do they appear to have an agenda? Are you able to identify the

STUDENTS: WHO CONNECTS YOUR DOTS?

agenda? Is there political motivation? Are they overlooking, ignoring, or leaving out information contrary to their desire? Are they using persuasive, or even deceptive, language? Are they showing emotion in their request? Are they using manipulative tactics?

Is there some way to challenge their view with an opposing viewpoint? What information can you draw from this? What questions can you ask them in order to gain more understanding of the situation? How can you become fully aware of the basis of the request?

Ask yourself questions and critically think about the information you gathered. However, *do not confuse* parenting for your safety with a manipulative political agenda! What conclusions have you reached based on the information?

This is just the tip of the iceberg. There are many additional ways in which your freedom is slipping away. Recall the massive iceberg that is said to have taken down the Titanic. Most of this structure dwelled hidden in the depths of the same icy, dark waters it rested upon, yet was capable of enormous devastation against many odds. Just as an iceberg is deceiving, it is also possible for information to be obscured, or even deluded, from the sphere of content made available to you while a multitude of hidden agendas lies beneath the surface…literally!

Take time to ask questions, perform research, and see the same things from a different perspective. Question the research and challenge the validity of it. Know when it's time to pick your battles and dig a little deeper rather than take things at face value. You can't go wrong by discovering more.

If you are influenced to think the way others think
without first thinking for yourself, are you really free?
—Jill Fandrich

The most effective way to destroy people is to deny and obliterate their own understanding of their history.
—George Orwell

Don't be a follower; be a thinker. Don't be a sheep; be a shepherd. Think for yourself and lead the way.
—Jill Fandrich

 Reflect:

1. Who is connecting your dots? Are you surprised by who or what it is? What changes will you make as a result of the revelation?
2. Watch or listen to different news sources (with different owners) and consider both sides of the same story. What is the basis for each opposing view?
3. Question social media content and research facts about a topic before formulating an opinion. Is there censoring involved? What have you discovered?
4. How can you gain more control over your thoughts and actions?
5. Define your moral code by which you evaluate incoming information. Use this basis to ask questions when presented with information.
6. How do you choose educational or entertainment sources? Where do you research the basis of the content? Do you realize that students are targets for educational manipulation? How can you verify the intent of the content?
7. Identify your core values and incorporate them into your mind's programming. What steps will you take to do this?
8. How can you protect yourself from conformity?

9. Identify the ways your freedom is being snatched. What other ways can you think of in which freedom is slipping away from you? What are your thoughts regarding this?

CHAPTER 3

Who's Hyped?

FEAR has been known to stand for *False-Events-Appearing-Real*. When a situation arises and fear creeps in, ask yourself CT questions. What is the source of the fear? What seems to be the reasoning for this fear? What appears to be the desired results of instilling fear in someone? Who does this benefit? Does *it* have an agenda? Has the source of the fear overlooked, ignored, or left out information that doesn't support its agenda? Is the source using unnecessary language to cause this fear? Is there a financial incentive for "the source"? Often, as a part of the manipulation, the content or discussions become heated and emotionally driven. An entirely new round of CT questions has evolved from the situation.

What causes people to blindly fall into a herd mentality without questioning the details behind it all? One method, as old as time yet obviously still effective, is intimidation by *fear*. If you scare people enough, you can exert control over them, even to the point that they hide their faces while alone and seclude themselves from public interaction.

That is a very severe depiction, yet a very real example, of what the world experienced in 2020 and the following years. In 2018 or 2019, would you ever have imagined willingly abandoning all outside activity, including your commute to school, and "hiding" indoors from something that cannot even be seen? When you instill enough fear into people, they become willing to abandon critical thought and fall prey to the control of the ones leading the charge.

How did the media participate in this event? Who funded the media? Is the media guilty of "outrage"? Observe all of the volatile words they use to gain control over you and your emotions while attempting to influence and control you. Words such as *outrage, corrupt, attacks, urgent,* and phrases like a *witch hunt, last chance, breaking news,* etc. These words and phrases are all designed to appeal to your emotions and cause you to *submit* to their authority. They are meant to spark fear to cease your ability to think critically and use logic. Do you want to be constantly "riled up" by such words? How would your health be affected if you were continually inflamed? Why do they feel they must strike you with emotional words to win your attention? *If "the source" actually believed in its own cause, manipulation wouldn't be needed.* Do you feel the media's agenda is more important to them than you are as a person deserving of the truth and the ability to think for yourself and make your own sound decisions based on facts?

Has there ever been a school-related or any other circumstance where you found yourself caught up in "all the hype"?

Ways to avoid getting caught up in the hype:

1. *By becoming mindfully aware.* It all begins with awareness. Take a step back, or maybe two, and assess the situation. Be mindful of the source of information. Who is causing the hype? What seems to be the reason for this happening? What appears to be the desired end result of the hype? How could this change things? Whom does this hype benefit?

    Does the source of this information appear to have an agenda? What is its agenda? Who is funding the source? Is the source overlooking, ignoring, or leaving out information that doesn't support its beliefs or claims? Is the source censoring people if they present with differing viewpoints? Is the source using persuasive or intimidating language to sway your perception? Is it relying on its ability to ignite your emotions in order for it to hook your attention and reel you into its side? Is it just trying to share unbiased and informative facts, or is it emotionally charged in its approach? What does it appear its goal is for you? To arouse your emotions?

Ask yourself questions about the situation and make yourself aware of as much information as possible. Be open to all angles and possibilities. You may still agree to side with it after critically thinking, but at least allow yourself to consider the occurrence from an unbiased perspective, asking questions in the process. Be aware of how it has chosen to engage with you.

2. *By meditating.* Take time to regain control of your senses and emotions. Now that you are aware of what they are attempting to do, take some deep breaths and find a way to relax. There are many effective methods of meditation to choose from. Find a quiet and serene room to calm yourself and bring yourself to a peaceful high-frequency vibration. Clear your thoughts of all biases and prejudices, and come to a place of honest contentment. Let your mind rest, and let your positive energy expand. Practice and explore various forms of meditation until you find the one that works best for you.

3. *By praying.* Just as you are able to clear your mind with meditation, you can clear your mind by focusing on your Creator and praising Him for all of your blessings. Place your trust in Him and the name of Jesus Christ. *"Let go and let God,"* as the saying goes. Be thankful for all that you have and are able to do. Praise and gratitude are two powerful qualities that can bring you to a place of tranquility in His precious name. Thank God for your freedom and ability to think critically without bias.

Conversationally, talk to God, and know He is with you at all times and through every event you encounter. Lean on Him, and nail your fears and concerns to the cross of Jesus Christ. Allow the peace beyond all understanding to flow through every cell of your body.

STUDENTS: WHO CONNECTS YOUR DOTS?

Pray for discernment as you wade through the ever-changing waters you encounter daily. Many wonderful prayers can be found online on every topic imaginable. Discover which prayers flow the best for you, or create your own. Let the Holy Spirit be your guide.

4. *By critically thinking.* Ask yourself questions regarding the situation, as discussed previously in this chapter. Who is doing what? What seems to be the reason for the situation happening? What are the desired end results? How could this change things? Who does this benefit?

   Does the source of this hyped information appear to have an agenda? What is the underlying agenda? Is the source overlooking, ignoring, or leaving out information that does not support its beliefs or claims? Is the source using unnecessary persuasive language to sway an audience's perception of the fact? Is it healthy for you to run on an "outraged" point of view? Does it benefit you or your family? Is it beneficial to your education or future?

   What might the consequences be if you submit to the intimidation of the hype? What purpose would this serve? Do they care for your well-being? What causes people to use intimidation as a method of influence? Is it an ethical way to "try to get your way"? Is it self-serving? Are there any other ways to interpret the message? What are the details of the opposing view?

   Perform extensive research on this and any other additional unbiased questions that come to mind. Analyze this information, verifying that the sources are valid and credible. Determine the relevance of the collected information and draw your own conclusion based on the unbiased, raw data.

5. *By stopping the flow of information.* Turn the television off. Close the news app, Internet, YouTube coverage, social media platforms, or other flow of hyped information. Is there a certain person trying to draw you into an emotional

state? Is there another source of information you can choose that is unbiased and not emotionally based? Perhaps you could back away from the information altogether?

Challenge yourself to shut off the valve of all emotionally-based sources for a week. Assess the condition of your mind after this week. Assess your emotions. Do you notice any difference? Perhaps try for two weeks—monitor, or even journal, regarding the results.

6. *By believing.* What is your belief system? Who do you believe in? Is this method aligned with your belief system? Do you feel a sense of tranquility at the thought of pursuing the hyped message? Your beliefs should lead you to a trusting place of serenity. Does this lead you there?

    Focus on your beliefs and let them direct your choices. Focus on what is good and what you know to be right and true. Do not let others intimidate or influence you under false pretenses. Know your core values, and let this be your guide. Define them and align with them. Put any questions you have through the CT process.

7. *By distractions.* What is important to you? Is it more important to focus on your family or your friends? How about a hobby you enjoy? Is there a venue you could serve in to help others? There are many activities you could engage in that are more productive than allowing the hype to consume you. Pour your heart and soul into your education, family, friends, church, or community service.

    Evaluate your priorities and disengage from the emotionally harmful noise. Where can you be a blessing to others? Who can you positively impact? How can you leave an enlightened footprint in this world?

Misery loves company, and a potential goal of the news outlets, hyped sources, or even a gossiper is to combine and *conform* as many people as possible, as there is power in persuasion. Once you add the factor of fear, you now have *control* as well.

STUDENTS: WHO CONNECTS YOUR DOTS?

In that same mindset, isn't it time to band together (yet as individuals) with like-minded people in your own crusade, aligned with your values and for the right reasons, to protect your own freedoms? It is time to take action. Too much time has been spent in blind ignorance, closing eyes to the rapidly changing and progressing movement, erasing history, and living by fear and discontentedness, always looking for a reason to be highly sensitized. It's time to become fully aware of what you now must face and the battle for your individual freedom.

CT requires that your knowledge is constantly updated as you take in new information. You must look at your own biases and be logical in your reasoning. Look at things for yourself. Make *your own* decisions, and be able to see more than one side of every issue.

Take the emotion away and think of the facts at hand. Carefully listen to the input of others and consider, yet know yourself enough to make your own independent, informed, and logical decision. Be open-minded while using truth-seeking reasoning. There is an art to being able to disconfirm the claims of others but done in such a way as to promote a common bond or shared fate. This would result in an *intensely* more powerful influence than by intimidation or deceit.

Use your mind without prejudice or fear, and learn to see things from opposing viewpoints. Evaluate information from different perspectives, be open-minded for consideration, yet stand firm in your final, unbiased conclusion. Think for yourself, and *never* stop asking questions.

> *Sometimes, the most powerful thing you*
> *can do is not get emotionally involved.*
> —Jill Fandrich

> *Stay grounded and avoid getting swept up*
> *in the hype, for it is in the calm and clarity*
> *of mind that true wisdom is found.*
> —Jill Fandrich

There is an art to being able to disconfirm the claims of others but done in such a way as to promote a common bond or shared fate.

—Jill Fandrich

 Reflect:

1. Think about a topic that strikes an emotion. Now engage in CT, and ask yourself a series of questions regarding that topic with an open mind and without prejudice. What do you notice? What insights have you discovered?
2. How do you avoid getting caught up in a "hyped" situation? What else can you add to this list?
3. How can you become more aware of potential manipulation in your environment? Can you remove your bias and listen open-mindedly, considering opposing vantage points? Explain.
4. How do you use distractions to "break away" from emotionally charged information? What other distractions can you think of?
5. How often do you listen to news sources? Have you ever found yourself caught up in the emotion? Describe a time you or someone you know was caught up emotionally. What did you learn about these situations? How did they end? What would you do differently now?
6. Have you ever encountered a "hyped" scenario regarding school? Describe the event. How was it resolved? What other ways could it have been resolved?

CHAPTER 4

How Do You Decide?

You are intelligent and able to process large amounts of information. You have a tremendous ability to think and consider multiple, and even complex, situations and potential responses. This separates you from other creatures, and each person has the opportunity to be authentic and think for him or herself. So, how do you take advantage of this opportunity? What is your primary mode of decision-making? Do you have a hunger or drive for something? Or maybe it is based on a need or outside influence? Why might you be affected by the influence of others? Let's examine possible methods.

Methods of decision-making:

1. *Critical thinking.* This is the desired method of decision-making. As mentioned, CT is a multi-faceted method of asking unbiased questions from different angles of a situation. After identifying the situation or issue, gather facts and relevant information in an untainted manner and consider more than one vantage point. Without prejudice, seek to discover and collect content before formulating an educated inference.

    Be sure to collect as much information as possible and to ascertain the credibility of the sources you used for research and the relevance of the contents. Understand the reasons why you are drawn to one viewpoint versus another. Is there an influential reason?

With CT, you want to be a "blank slate" as you gather the data. Yet, as you have thoroughly processed all potential avenues, bring forth your innate sense of right and wrong as a guide, along with your carefully chosen objective evidence, in drawing a conclusion. Allow logic and common sense to be your GPS, and navigate to a decision that is emotion-free in its origins.

2. *Intimidation.* Unfortunately, many things in life become, or perhaps always have been, intimidating. As you progress through different stages of life, the object of intimidation may change, yet there will likely be intimidating factors lurking. What comes to mind as an intimidating factor in your life? Or possibly, who? When you hear the word intimidation, what instinctively comes to mind? Is it a person, a group, a location, a status, or maybe a situational event? How do you handle intimidation? Do you give in to the influence and allow your values to be compromised? Or do you proceed with your own agenda despite it?

Are some situations more intimidating than others? How do they affect you? Do you allow intimidation to control how you make decisions?

How can you build up a tolerance against intimidation? How can you avoid intimidating people or circumstances? Prepare yourself to remain strong and convicted in your values, notwithstanding any attempts from others of intimidation. If possible, attempt to view things from both perspectives and consider all possibilities.

Analyze all information you gathered through trusted sources, and draw your own conclusions from the data at hand. Ultimately, critically think through intimidating factors, and do not allow them to compromise your values.

3. *Reputation.* Are you influenced by how people perceive you? This is very common in younger generations, as proven

by social media, yet it can be influential to young and old alike. It is human nature to want to be accepted by others. But is this a factor so powerful in your life that you will allow it to be a determining factor in making decisions? In particular, what if a morality issue was on the line? Would you base your decision regarding the issue on observing your conscience, or would you base it on how you will "look best" on social media?

How much time do you spend on social media? Do you focus on your number of followers or how many people respond to "like" something you have posted? What causes the opinions of "social media" participants to value this digital form of acceptance more than in-person comradery? Do you partake for fun with no influential concern for responses, or do you rely on interactions for a form of popularity or acceptance?

How about in a school setting? Do you make decisions a certain way due to your reputation? How about settings such as social or family situations or any other setting? Does your reputation in any setting affect how you make decisions? Do you, or are you willing to, compromise your values for your reputation?

4. *Herd mentality.* There truly is power in numbers, and inhibitions can also be altered. Some people feel "safe" when they are within a group and may be inclined to "become" what they are all about. A good example of this is found in "gangs." The premise of a gang is to find security in a group of people and feel accepted. In the process, the group generally thinks as one unit—group-think—in the hopes and expectations of acceptance.

Often, they may not even be *permitted* to think for themselves. They lost their individuality and gave in to conformity. Possibly, at this point, there may even be a *penalty* if they attempt to leave the group.

There are many other groups of like-minded people as well. Some are advantageous, and some are harmful. In a group, it is important to have the freedom and safety to still think and speak for yourself. Are you permitted to be authentic? Do you follow in line with the majority? Who benefits from being in the group? Who controls the group? What are your reasons for being in the group?

Do you consider all information and then formulate your own opinion? How do you respond if the majority is in agreement that violates your opinion, code, or morals? If you respond with an opposing view, how do they respond to you? Would you still be accepted? Or would you be in danger? Is the group mellow or volatile? What seems to be the agenda of the group? Are you strong enough to stand up for your beliefs and make independent decisions?

5. *Peer pressure.* Peer pressure is often a concern for students. It can, however, also exist in other venues as well. The premise of peer pressure, like herd mentality, is also the desire to be accepted by others. Sometimes, you may be challenged to do something or act in a certain way based on the promptings of someone else. Perhaps it is a peer, friend, stranger, a "cyberbully," or even someone in authority. It could stem from a group of friends or even family.

Whatever the source, how are you affected by pressure from peers? Who is applying the pressure? What seems to be the desired goal of the pressure? How does the pressure affect your ability to make decisions? Do you allow them to influence you and sway your decisions? Do you consider the validity of their request or insistence?

Identify the situation, and allow yourself to listen to their side of the issue. Consider the source, and if more information is needed to substantiate the claim, perform your own research. Find out as many facts regarding the situation as possible. Evaluate all of the data.

Next, align the information with your values. What are potential options to resolve the situation? Independently draw your own conclusions. Did you come to the same conclusions as they did, using an unbiased CT method? If your conclusion differs, are you confident enough to stand firm in your decision, which aligns with your values? How can you gain more confidence, if needed, to stand up for your beliefs?

What types of pressures from other people affect you? What are some ways you can avoid peer pressure in the first place? How can you create an environment where peer pressure is minimized, if not eliminated, altogether?

6. *Financial advantage.* Financial incentives are intriguing and, most likely, appealing. But what is the premise of the incentive? Is it in exchange for a worthy service, object, or event? Or is there a persuasive nature, requesting you to sway to a certain side of an issue? How might you be influenced by a financial persuasion, even if it is set against your sense of what is right? Or are you able to choose the "right" option despite a prosperous reward for choosing the "wrong" side?

Is there a dollar amount that is a deciding factor? Are there any other extenuating circumstances that would lead to a decision based on a financial advantage? How would you handle a significantly prosperous request that clashed with your morals? What if it compromised your safety or the safety of someone else? How can you guard yourself against allowing a financial incentive to sway your decisions when your values or safety are concerned?

7. *Fear.* Fear encompasses numerous possibilities, each different for every individual. What are some of your fears? What is your biggest fear? Do you have a fear of rejection or of being alone? Do you have a fear of missing out on something (fomo)? Or maybe a general fear, such as a fear of the unknown? There may be a fear derived from

not being accepted or perhaps a fear of harm if you don't conform to a certain way or opinion.

Identify your greatest fear. How would this fear shape the way you make decisions if it came into play? Would it cause you to decide differently if the fear was absent? Would it cause you to make a decision against your morals or belief system? Would any of your values be compromised?

How can you *reframe* this fear and see it in a new light? Is there any conditioning you can perform, or things to avoid, to desensitize, or even remove yourself from the fear? Identify ways to separate this fear from your decision-making opportunities.

8. *Emotionally charged.* An emotionally charged person, especially a group, could distinctly impact a situation. People who are emotionally charged often respond based on emotions rather than logic. It is difficult not to be affected by this type of volatile demeanor, especially if you are a well-controlled or gentle person. The negative vibrations are infectious and spread rapidly.

    Many movements today are actually *based* on emotions themselves rather than logic. How do you respond when you are with someone running on high emotions? Are you influenced to side with them just to keep the peace? Or maybe out of fear? How do you respond when you are in a highly charged group? Would you tend to conform to the intense energy? Are you still able to hold true to your beliefs? How would you handle the emotional intensity if it contrasted with your values?

    Identify ways to remove yourself from the emotion in this type of situation, and allow yourself to think critically to an unbiased resolution.

9. *Spiritually charged.* Sometimes, a spiritual aspect may draw people to a decision. It may not necessarily be based upon what is right versus wrong, but rather, it is *spiritually*

driven. This method may build on passion, a belief, or a desire, also with an emotional attachment.

How would you handle something of this persuasion? Do you still respond based on your core values? Perhaps it's a matter of "how" you respond that is of concern. Have you ever been overly passionate about a cause you believed in and responded in a way you normally wouldn't have? Do you let passion alter the way you respond? How might you respond if your beliefs were being jeopardized? Are you able to look at both sides indiscriminately?

What information can you gather that might help reach a logical conclusion? How can you hold your emotions at bay while looking unbiasedly at both sides? How can you avoid potential situations that contradict your values in the first place? Collect as much information as possible without prejudice, then draw a logical solution rather than "drinking the Kool-Aid."

10. *Loyalty.* Loyalty is an admirable character quality if it is aligned with your values. What or who are you loyal to? What are the reasons for the loyalty? To what extent will you devote your allegiance? What would you do if the object of your loyalty was compromised? How would you respond if you were challenged regarding your loyalty? Would your loyalty trump over values?

    What is the opposing perspective on the situation? Is there a reasonable premise? Will this cause you to alter how you respond? How far would you take loyalty when it coincides with your values? How far would you take it if it *contradicts* your values? If trust was broken, how would you handle the situation? Will your loyalty ever cause you to compromise your values? How does loyalty affect how you make decisions?

11. *Obedience.* Everyone is required to be obedient to someone during their lifetime, and generally, quite a few people. To whom are you required to be obedient? Would obedience

to an authority figure affect your decision to do something *against* your values? What about obedience to someone you trust and love? Could that possibly lead you to compromise your values?

Is there a scenario that would cause you to go against your belief system in the name of obedience? Are you obedient without question? Or do you think critically while using your values in making a decision? Where and to what extent does your obedience lie?

Gather as much information as necessary in such a situation to provide the proper knowledge to make your decisions. Be prepared to perform detailed research before ever blindly obeying an authority that lies *opposite* your values. How can you prepare for times like this? How does obedience affect your decision-making process? Ensure your values are clearly defined.

12. *Need- or desire-based.* Do you allow a need or desire to compromise your decisions? Will you go against your beliefs to satisfy a need? What about a desire? Are you willing to alter a decision and go against your values to attain an object in need or one you "want"?

    Perhaps there are some you would and some you would not. How would you handle these types of situations? What are some of your strong needs or desires? How do you evaluate their importance compared to your values?

    Do you consider your values and make a logical decision? Do you have control over your wants and needs? If not, what can you do to gain control over them? How will you compare opposing sides and evaluate these situations unbiasedly if appropriate? How do your needs and desires affect your decision-making process?

13. *Insecurity.* Many forms of insecurities have the potential to influence decisions. Insecurity, in general, can lead people to act in peculiar ways. Perhaps you want to be liked, accepted, or to stand out as unique. Or maybe you don't

want to stand out in a crowd. Perhaps it is based on a talent or the work that you do.

Have you ever let an insecurity sway a decision that you made? What was the premise of the insecurity? Who was involved? Who benefited from this decision? Is there a certain insecurity that would cause you to set aside your values? What would you do if the insecurity presented itself, even though you would not be harmed, by choosing your values? Are you stronger than your insecurity? How can you find out more information regarding opposing sides of the insecurity?

Collect as much information as possible, then evaluate the data. How can you work toward resolving the insecurity so it is no longer an issue? How can you prepare so insecurity is not an issue when making decisions?

14. *Past experience.* It is common to base how you currently make decisions on past experiences. More often than not, this is the most effective and predictable way to proceed. As new information arises, however, this is a great opportunity to think critically about how an alternate approach may or may not be considered.

Consider the risks and benefits of utilizing what is known from past experiences versus the new information presented. Ask yourself unbiased questions and be open to new possibilities through logical reasoning while still considering the effectiveness of past processes. Critically think of opposing views and thoroughly research using reputable sources if applicable. Perform your research independently, resisting conformity. Use your own logic to reach your own individual conclusions without bias or influence from anyone else. What have you decided?

There are many different factors behind the process of making a decision. Perhaps you have encountered half, or even all, of the previous conditions at some point in your life. No matter what you are experiencing or how you approach the decision, employ CT methods before you make your ultimate decisions.

What is the situation? Who is involved? What are your options? Who will be affected by your decision? How will you or they be affected? Could anyone get hurt in the process? Whom does this benefit? Will your decision be something you can be proud of? How will the decision shape your reputation or future? How will the decision grow you as a person? What are the potential consequences for each decision option available? What is the right thing to do? What is this based on? What obstacles might be clouding your judgment? What option will lead to the best possible outcome? What decision will be best for your legacy? How did you reach your final decision? What are other potential responses? Are you allowing other people or things to affect your decision? Are you using logic?

Utilizing credible and reliable resources, research and gather as much relevant information as possible. Analyze and extrapolate your own conclusions based on the raw data.

> *We all make choices, but in the end, our choices make us.*
> —Ken Levine

> *Good and evil both increase at compound interest. That is why the little decisions you and I make every day are of such infinite importance.*
> —C.S. Lewis

> *Critical thinking is the key to making wise decisions. It allows us to evaluate the information at hand, consider different perspectives, and make informed choices that align with our values and goals.*
> —Jill Fandrich

 Reflect:

1. What is your primary mode of decision-making? Name factors that could affect how you make your decisions.
2. Name someone you know who practices CT in his or her decision-making opportunities. How does this process affect their decision outcomes?
3. How can you incorporate more CT and less influential distractions into your decisions?
4. Think of a time when you allowed intimidation to affect your decision-making. How can you reframe this by critically thinking? What would you do differently?
5. How about a situation involving your reputation? Herd-mentality? Peer pressure? Financial advantage? Fear? Emotionally charged? Spiritually charged? Loyalty? Obedience? Need- or desire-based? Insecurity? Past experience? How can you reframe each of these methods by thinking critically?
6. Describe a time when you had a difficult decision to make. How did you process the situation? What were things you considered? Were you easily persuaded? What would you now do differently?
7. How can you become less influenced by others?

CHAPTER 5

Healthy Relationships

Family

Relationships are different for everyone. It is human nature to want and need interaction with other people. This starts with your family. It is important to have strong bonds with family, whether you are a biological son or daughter, adopted or even fostered. The way you were brought up has a significant impact on your life and the choices you make. Not everyone may have a healthy or even ideal childhood, which is very unfortunate. Everyone does, however, have the ability to process their childhood and make decisions on how to respond to the present moment and future ones as well. Never allow yourself to feel like a victim of your circumstances. It is your *responses* that define you. How are you currently responding to situations? Is it effective? Are you making rational decisions based on logic and sound reasoning? Or do you tend to have knee-jerk reactions? What is the right thing to do? Do you need to make any changes? What do you do correctly? What could you do better?

Exodus 20:12 ESV instructs you, *"Honor your father and your mother, that your days may be long in the land that the LORD your God is giving you."* Never let yourself fall into a "victim mentality." Honor those who raise you, even if you disagree with them. Instead, grow, learn, adjust, and make amends or logical changes if necessary to move forward healthily and favorably.

Describe your childhood. Do you feel it was or is healthy? Do you add positive or negative energy to your family? How can you be more instrumental in extending positivity and kindness to your family? How do your decisions affect family members? Do you consider how they may be affected when you make decisions? Have you hurt any of them based on decisions you made? Do you make decisions you and your family can be proud of? Do your decisions affect your reputation or that of your family? Has anyone in your family ever made a decision that negatively affected or hurt you? If so, describe this situation. Remember, parents have many difficult decisions to make, and while not all may appear desirable to you, they are generally made in your best interest. Your parents are looking out for your safety and long-term success.

How can you resolve the hurt feelings that exist from areas of disagreement and move forward with forgiveness? Protecting your family's bond and name is a big responsibility. Also, choose to honor and respect your parents and protect the health of your family connection and reputation.

What do you know about forgiveness? Do you practice this regularly? Does your family practice forgiveness? How can forgiveness shared in a family heal emotional wounds? How can you learn more about forgiveness and its healing properties? Apply CT to decisions you make in your choices that affect your family.

When it comes to your family, what obstacles tend to cloud your judgment? What are ways you could avoid or go around the obstacles? How can you deal directly with obstacles? How can you inject more fun or unity into your family time? Value the blessing of having a family and your lifelong connection with them. Praise and thank God for the gift of your family. In what ways can you show more love and gratitude for your family? What are you already doing well? How can you improve the love and forgiveness you show them? Psalm 127:3 NASB confirms, *"Behold, children are a gift of the LORD. The fruit of the womb is a reward."*

Does your family have a designated "Family Night"? What traditions do you carry out? How do you celebrate holidays? What are ways you can be more supportive of family time? Do you engage with your siblings or parents at mealtime? Do you share chores and help each other with them? In what ways can you make chore time a more pleasant event? How can you show more appreciation for your family? Do you spend time with other relatives? How many relatives do you have? Are you close to any of them?

What questions can you ask when it comes to making decisions that involve your family? What things do you consider? What are your options? Who will be affected by your decisions? Apply the CT process and prioritize the health of your family's bond.

> *Other things may change us, but we start and end with the family.*
> —Anthony Brandt

Friends

It is important to have close friendships in your life. Do not fall into the social media trap of thinking that the more "followers" you have, the more friends you actually have, or the more popular you are. Having even just a few *very* close friends in your lifetime is more important. The number may vary, but the point is to have *unconditional* friends you can always count on and who can count on you. Always put quality over quantity when it comes to friends. Do not allow any biases from others to affect the devotion to each other. True friends will reciprocate this loyalty. A friend will be there for you in your successes, failures, and troubles, when in need, and when they or you have plenty. How do you show gratitude and respect for your friends?

One Thessalonians 5:11 NIV says, *"Therefore encourage one another and build each other up, just as in fact you are doing."* And regarding a friend who is not true, *"Do not be misled: 'Bad company corrupts good character,"* 1 Corinthians 15:33 NIV. Ecclesiastes 4:10 NIV teaches you, *"If either of them falls down, one can help the other up. But pity anyone who falls and has no one to help them up."* Value the blessing of a friend. Be selective as you choose your friends and align with those who share your values. Connect with people moving in the same direction as you, with similar goals, values, and qualities.

STUDENTS: WHO CONNECTS YOUR DOTS?

Do not be unequally yoked together with unbelievers.
For what fellowship has righteousness with lawlessness?
And what communion has light with darkness?
—2 Corinthians 6:14 (NKJV)

Much of your influence in life will come from the people you choose to be around. It may be while in school, at work, participating in activities or events, or just nearby, such as in your neighborhood or dorm complex. Whomever you spend the most time with will have the greatest impact on your life. Make sure you choose wisely from whom this influence will come. You have the ability and responsibility to make this decision.

How can you be a good friend? How well do you listen to what others say? Do you interrupt when they are talking? Do you offer consoling words if warranted? How can you show compassion toward them? How do you make decisions when they are affected? How do you choose your friends? Why might it be important to align your friends with your values? What are some consequences of choosing carelessly? What methods will you use to decipher or ensure truthful information from friends? When it comes to true and lifelong friends, be selective and discover as much about them as possible. Choosing like-minded friends and prioritizing the relationship's health is important.

Sometimes, the people you trust the most are the ones likely to deceive you, even if unintentionally. You may be less likely to doubt seemingly good intentions. How can you still honor the friendship yet be cautious not to overlook your values or responsibilities? What questions can you ask yourself when a dilemma arises? How can you verify the validity of controversial information when a friend is involved and not let the friendship cloud your judgment? Is there a chance your friend may not have all the information to reach a logical or informed conclusion?

Have you ever had a friend try to lead you astray? What was the situation? What were your options? What did you choose to do? What was the outcome? Did you choose wisely? Why did you choose the way you did? What did you do correctly? What would you do differently next time? Are you easily influenced by your friends? Are you able to process information logically and objectively when a sensitive topic is involved?

Have you ever been "bullied"? What is bullying to you? Have you ever bullied anyone else? What was the scenario in either case? What were the choices or options involved? Was it a close friend or more of an acquaintance or peer? How did you handle the situation? How did you rationalize your choices? What did you do well? What would you change? How did you reach this decision?

How do you interpret information relayed to you from a friend? Do you trust it without verifying? Have you ever been misguided in this manner? Have you ever shared faulty information with a friend? How can you be sure of the facts involved? Have you ever had a good friend share information in good faith and with good intentions, but the information wasn't correct or complete? How can you discern the truthfulness of the content despite good intentions?

> *The righteous choose their friends carefully, but the way of the wicked leads them astray.*
> —Proverbs 12:26 NIV

> *As iron sharpens iron, so a friend sharpens a friend.*
> —Proverbs 27:17 NLT

> *A friend is always loyal, and a brother is born to help in time of need.*
> —Proverbs 17:17 NLT

> *Wounds from a friend can be trusted, but an enemy multiplies kisses.*
> —Proverbs 27:6 NIV

> *No one has greater love than this: to lay down his life for his friends.*
> —John 15:13 CSB

STUDENTS: WHO CONNECTS YOUR DOTS?

School

It is important and necessary to have interactions with other students. While hopefully, you develop close bonds with classmates, it is at least imperative to have a healthy working relationship and help and learn from each other. Knowledge is essential, and so is the process of learning. Every individual learns differently. Open your mind to learning new things or simply new ways of learning from other students. Share with them what you know and what you find works the best for you. Listen to them regarding what works best for them. What have you learned from them? Avoid becoming emotional if someone doesn't share the same opinion as you. Instead, value that person and accept the differences in views. It doesn't mean you have to agree. Rather, you may learn something new in the process. Be open-minded.

Develop symbiotic relationships of helping each other, and hopefully some lifetime bonds as well. How do you make decisions while in a school or class setting? What is the topic or situation? Who is involved? What are your options? How will other students be affected by your decisions or choices? Could anyone get hurt in the process? How could you help someone in the process? Could your decision be something you would be proud of? How will your decision grow you or another student as a person? What are the potential consequences of each option available? What is the right thing to do? What obstacles might be clouding your judgment? What decision will be best for your legacy? How did you reach your final decision?

What are some scenarios involving other students where you have decisions to make? How about the same questions involving a teacher or professor? What other questions come to mind in each of these situations? What other things might you need to consider? What method of decision-making makes the most sense? How can you begin to stand out as a leader in your role as a student? How do you interact with an authority figure, such as a teacher? Are you open and teachable? Are you respectful and responsive? How can you set a good example for others to follow? Do other students easily influence you? Or are you the influencer? Ask yourself and others questions to learn more about what is being said and by whom.

Have you ever found yourself in a situation where another student acted out as a bully? What was the situation? How did you respond? What are other options on how to respond? Who else should know about this occurrence? How might sharing this situation with others prevent someone else from being hurt as well? What are some logical ways to resolve this situation or future interactions with this person? Where can you find out more information about this topic? It is important to find a resolution to this rather than avoid the situation. Involve others where possible and diligently work toward a resolution to promote a healthy and safe environment for learning, growth, and development. There is no place for this type of behavior in this or any other type of environment.

A successful future starts now in your interactions with other students, teachers, and instructors. Be the first to listen, lend a hand, and offer your time. Respond to instructions and be attentive to those sharing information with you. Be available to meet the needs of others. It's wise to ask questions and find out more. Perhaps even challenge the information, but with an open mind for truth, seeking discovery from opposing sides of an argument. These are qualities of successful people, and the more these skills are practiced, the more they are a part of you and are programmed into your mind. You will find that if you practice them enough, you are on your way to becoming a *captivating* person and leader. Make it a point to embrace these skills and allow them to be an example to others.

Another area for CT consideration not to be overlooked is the *content* of the educational information. Is there a political agenda involved in the "academic" material? Be aware that education is intended to be a sharing of instructional and informational content without a sociopolitical agenda. Ask yourself CT questions when it comes to content, and think critically about the intent of the content. Is it intended to instruct objectively, or is persuasion involved? Is there an underlying bias or manipulation? More about this topic is found in other chapters.

STUDENTS: WHO CONNECTS YOUR DOTS?

How else can you positively influence and promote healthy relationships with other students or academic personnel?

Work-related

Relationships are also formed in a work setting. You have or will develop certain interactions with your boss as well as your other superiors and coworkers. It is important to have open and honest communication with them all. Be teachable and ready to step up to the plate with full responsibility and initiative. Ask questions to gain an understanding of your role and how you can help your boss and the company. Use logic and be a team player. Be selective and verify the values of the company you wish to work for before applying for a position. What do they stand for? Who do they serve? What is their mission? What are their values? Do your values align with that of the company? Thoroughly research the company beforehand to determine if its values and mission align with your belief system.

What is your position? What are the responsibilities of your position? You should have received a *Job Description* that outlines your duties. Do you understand everything included? If not, what will you do to find out more information? Is there someone else in your same position? How can you improve? What changes can you make to be the best at what you do? No matter your position, strive to be the best in every detail you perform. Make it a habit to work toward excellence in all that you do. Make it a goal every day to do better than the day before. Who else can you assist? What did you do well? What could you improve upon?

How is your relationship with your boss? Is there more than one boss or superior? How many coworkers do you work with? Do you get along with them all? If not, is it because of something you are doing or have done? Either way, what changes could improve this situation and help establish a healthy environment? What would this entail? If you do get along well, is there anything you can do to promote more teamwork or unity? Can you be the one to initiate positive ideas or changes? How can you stand out positively as an example to others?

Is there someone you can think of who is struggling? What can you do right now to help? Are you providing compassion and encouragement where appropriate? These are things that can be done with anyone who is challenged in some way. How else could you help? How do you determine what the need may be? How do you initiate a conversation in a new interaction? How do you maintain good and healthy work relationships? Be the first to lend a hand and lead by example. What other ideas come to mind?

Toxic relationships

Have you ever experienced a toxic relationship? How would you define a toxic relationship? What characteristics stand out to you? What are the warning signs? Are you currently in a toxic relationship? This could be in a family, friend, school, work, or personally-related area. Toxic people are everywhere, and they always will be. It is vital to learn how to identify different types of toxic people and personalities and either avoid them or learn how to respond to them and part ways, unaffected by the interaction.

Sometimes, you will find yourself entangled with a toxic person. Perhaps there is a student with a strong, arrogant personality, and you must complete an assignment with them. Or maybe it is a family member or coworker you need to work on a project with. What's important is to be aware of the toxicity and have the ability to think critically about the scenario and the toxic person. Then, make logical and objective decisions in your interactions. It is difficult to have a "healthy relationship" with a toxic person. However, you can learn to make it as amicable as possible.

Is there any truth to what they are saying? Are they speaking logically? What is the topic of their conversation? Is it relevant to the circumstance? Do they appear to have an underlying message or ulterior motive? Do they seem to have an agenda? Are they subjective rather than objective? Be prepared to think critically and question your way to an unbiased position of truth in the matter. It is important to remain unbiased and not to let your emotions cloud your judgment.

STUDENTS: WHO CONNECTS YOUR DOTS?

Whenever possible, avoid toxic people. If it isn't possible, learn to set boundaries, especially regarding these people. It is good to have your boundaries defined in advance and know your limits. What are your boundaries? How do you define them? How can you enforce them? Never let a toxic person, or anyone else for that matter, cross your line under any circumstance. Research in advance and learn as much as you can about toxic people, especially if you know someone in particular you must interact with. How will you respond to them in a future interaction? How can you prepare?

Healthy relationships are vital to a fulfilled life. Every encounter you have is an opportunity for a relationship. You have the ability to choose whether it is a good interaction or an unfavorable one. Learn how to interact well with people and think critically about each one. Why has this interaction occurred? How should you respond? What might be learned or could be shared? Is there someone you could help in the process? Is there a need you have the opportunity to help? Is there a connection to be made? Are you cordial and inviting? Are you professional and brief? Are you relaxed and pleasant? How do you know which way to approach each interaction? Where can you learn more about how to think critically about healthy relationships?

The love of a family is life's greatest blessing,
and nurturing healthy family relationships
is essential to happiness and fulfillment.
—Jill Fandrich

Healthy school friendships are the foundation for a
positive and supportive learning environment where
students can thrive both academically and emotionally.
—Jill Fandrich

Good relationships are the foundation of
a healthy work environment. They create
a culture of trust, communication, and
collaboration, which are essential for success.
—Jill Fandrich

Surround yourself with people who reflect who you want to be and how you want to feel; energies are contagious.
—Rachel Wolchin

 **Reflect:**

1. Name someone you know who has a healthy family relationship. What does a healthy relationship look like?
2. What are your thoughts about your relationship with your family? What are you doing right? Where can you improve? How will you do this? Describe your relationship with your family.
3. Name someone you know who has healthy friendships. What do they look like? Describe your friendships.
4. Name three scenarios when you could use the comfort of a valued and trustworthy friend.
5. Think of students who have a knack for getting along with everyone. What makes them stand out? What skills do you identify them using? Do you utilize these same skills? What are you doing correctly? What changes could you make to be more effective?
6. Name someone who has healthy work-related relationships. How does this affect their performance? If you currently work, what are your relationships like at your job?
7. Describe toxic personalities. Have you experienced a toxic person before? What are some of the characteristics? How did you interact with this person? What did you do correctly? What improvements could you make? How can you better prepare for future interactions with a toxic person?
8. How can you incorporate more critical thinking and less influential distractions into your relationship decisions?

STUDENTS: WHO CONNECTS YOUR DOTS?

9. Analyze all of your most important relationships. Are they healthy? If not, what changes can you make?
10. What have you learned about healthy relationships? Have you identified anything you need to work on?

CHAPTER 6

Activities and Academics

Activities

There are many opportunities to participate in various activities, events, clubs, and societies. What interests you? Why do you find it interesting? Is it something just for fun? Is it something that will grow you morally? How about physically, personally, spiritually, or professionally? Will it develop your mental capacities? Are there any ways it could harm you? How do you know the answers to these questions?

How do you determine which activities are best for you? With each activity you consider, refer to Chapter 1 and the *CT Questions for Decision-Making*. What is the activity or event? What does it entail? Are there any restrictions or safety concerns? What is the club or society? What does it stand for? Is there some kind of underlying agenda? What can you do to find out this information?

Who is involved in the activity, event, club, or society? Who else are you considering when you think about engaging in it? Do you know the people? What do you know about the people? How well do you know the people? Where can you find out more about them? What else are they involved in? Do they have an obvious cause they represent?

What other options do you have? What else have you considered joining or attending? Is there a variety to choose from or a limited selection? Has this affected your decision? How do the options compare? What are you basing this on? What are the highlights of each one? What are the disadvantages of each one? Which one will challenge you the most? In what ways will you be challenged? Which one comes the easiest? What makes it easy? Why do you think that way?

Who will be affected by your decision? Are there a lot of people affected? How will you be affected by your decision? In what ways? Describe how deciding to participate in certain activities or events could affect you. Is it a positive or negative effect? Based on what? How will others be affected by your decision? Who will you discuss the possibilities with? Will you share your concerns with others? Is there anything you are afraid to mention? Or are you excited to mention it? Will it positively or negatively affect your schoolwork? Will your time be affected?

Could anyone get hurt in the process? Is it physically challenging? Will it put anyone, including yourself, at risk? Is it mentally hurtful for you or anyone else? Describe any areas where someone could be hurt in some capacity. Is there a way to easily resolve this? Is there a way to plan ahead for long-term safety? Who could help with this process? How can you ensure no one will be hurt due to your choice?

Will your decision be something you can be proud of? Will you be able to share with everyone what you selected or participated in? Do you consider how this will affect your loved ones? Will this be something they can be proud of? Do you consider them while making decisions?

How will you allow your decision to shape your reputation or future? Do you consider how your reputation will be affected by each decision you make? Do you understand that your reputation will follow you for life? How would you currently describe your reputation? How would you like to describe your future reputation? What will you do to protect it? Will any of the activities, events, clubs, or societies you are interested in impact your reputation or future? How do you know this? If you aren't sure, how can you find out?

How will your choice of involvement grow you as a person? In what ways? Describe the growth potential for all of your options. Which one stands out as the best? Which one appears to be the worst? How does this affect your decision? What kind of impact does it have? What character qualities could be developed with your involvement? Are there any potential bad traits? How can they be avoided?

What are the potential consequences for each decision option available? Are they good or bad? Which of them aligns with your goals and values? Which do not, and how do you know this? How will this affect your decision? Is anyone other than you affected by the consequences? Does the timing of the activity interfere with any other obligations?

What is the right thing to do? Is it an obvious decision? Which options stand out as appropriate? Which ones stand out as red flags? How can you tell? Describe the right ones. What makes them right? How often do you choose the right one? How often do you make the wrong choice? How do you respond when you make a bad decision? What are some consequences of bad decisions? How would this affect you?

What obstacles might cloud your judgment in your thought-processing of an activity, event, club, or society? Is there something influential swaying your decision? Is it a physical or mental obstacle? What are your thoughts about the obstacle? Is it a warning sign telling you to avoid something, or must you be creative to overcome the obstacle? Do you need to work on more skills or other preparation before you pursue it? What are the positive or negative consequences of being a part of it? Are you considering registering or applying for the right reasons? What are the reasons you are considering this? Is it something you really enjoy? If not, why? Do you feel pressured by this decision?

What option will lead to the best possible outcome? Which is the most fun? Which is the safest? Are any of them dangerous? Would being involved in any of them hurt you or anyone else? Will any of them grow you intellectually or broaden your horizons? Will they develop new life-long skills?

What activity, event, club, or society will be best for your legacy? Is it something you will be proud of for years to come? Can you imagine sharing stories about your choice with your grandparents, other relatives, or future spouse? Does it align with the reputation you want to build for yourself? Is there anything that doesn't feel right about it? If so, why is that? Is this something you can live with? Is there a better choice you can make? Does the opinion of others affect the way you reason?

STUDENTS: WHO CONNECTS YOUR DOTS?

How did you reach your final decision? What things did you consider before you made this decision? What questions did you ask yourself? What is important for you to consider before making this type of decision? Are you making the decision independently after considering all the mentioned questions?

Academics

Education is vital to any work-related position you can imagine. Whether you desire to be a mechanic, electrician, athlete, medical professional, attorney, teacher, firefighter, business owner, author, engineer, pilot, or truck driver, you must have certain skills to perform your job well. Take your education seriously. It should be a life-long venture. Never stop learning or shut yourself off from pertinent information. Be open to continuously gaining knowledge in as many areas as possible. Knowledge can be attained from all of your surroundings. Use your five senses to observe your environment and constantly be aware of how things work and operate.

Ask questions to fill in the blanks or expand on what you already know. Discover new ways of doing things you have been doing for years. You might learn how to complete something more efficiently or even more accurately.

How do you select which courses you enroll in? Are they prerequisites you do not have a say in? Are there some that are electives you may choose from? How do you make your decision? Are you influenced by anyone else? If so, whom? If not, what motivates you to make a selection? Are you thinking long-term, such as a future career? Do you think short-term and base it on who else may be in that class? Or is it specifically based on enjoyable content?

How do you see "academics" in general? Is it a tool to guide you to a promising future? Do you just want to get by with the bare minimum effort? What are you willing to contribute to learning? How important is gaining knowledge to you? What are you willing to sacrifice for a "good" education? What do you consider a "good" education? What are the benefits of education? What might be some consequences of not putting much effort into academics?

To you, does education need to be the only focus? Or do you prefer to simultaneously engage in other activities, such as a sport? What determines how you approach this? Are you able to manage your time and perform both to the best of your ability? Which comes first? How do you balance homework versus practices or meetings? Which is more important to you? How can you benefit from both at the same time?

How much time do you put into your studies? Do you ever read ahead in preparation? Do you actively participate in class? Do you take the lead on projects, whether in the classroom or an after-school group? Do you carry your share of the weight? Or maybe even more? Does learning come easily to you, or do you have to work really hard to get a concept to "stick"?

Have you ever let outside activities come before schoolwork? If so, when and what were they? Do you have any regrets? Would you do it again? What were the circumstances? What would you do differently? What did you do right?

How do you learn the best? Are you a good learner in a big, crowded auditorium? Or do you prefer a small class setting? How are you at taking the initiative for an online course? Are you able to keep up the pace and be self-motivated? It's important to discover how you learn best. Do you micro-record classes and listen again? Do you like to write down word-for-word what is said? Do you take general notes from the teachings? Do you read the section ahead of time? Do you study in a group or by yourself? Do you underline or use a highlighter? Do you use multiple colored highlighters and learn in a photographic sense? Do you use anacronyms or other creative ways to jog your memory? There are many different learning methods, and there is no one-size-fits-all system.

Take some time to discover how you learn the best. Everyone is unique and must identify how to learn the best method individually. The earlier you figure this out, the more benefits you will gain from a system that accentuates your best and most reliable method. Encourage others to develop the style that works best for them as well.

Where can a good education take you? What are some of your goals and dreams? How can you see education fitting into their pathway? Write down a list of your goals and a separate list of your dreams. Read these lists daily and always consider what it will take to reach them. How you prepare today will be a step in your progression to reaching them faster and with the necessary preparation so you are fully equipped to succeed. Each day, add any new ideas that may facilitate the steps of how to achieve the goals and dreams. Be analytical and calculated as you describe your ideas in detail. Let this be an ongoing list that is "alive" and reviewed daily. What gets written down is more likely to occur than what isn't. Plus, your mind constantly works subconsciously as you routinely consider these goals and dreams.

What are your thoughts about future education? As mentioned, learning should be a lifelong process as you continually research information on a day-to-day basis. How do you fix this or operate that? Research today is easier than ever before and is right at your fingertips—literally. Take advantage of how easily information can be found. Also, be cautious regarding how deceitful some information can be. As you are learning throughout this course, only use credible sources and block all unnecessary or explicit content that is nothing but a harmful temptation. Be selective and be able to discern if the information is biased, misleading, emotionally based, influential, prejudiced, subjective, or in some way meant to sway your opinion. Use CT methods as you select how and what to educate yourself with.

Education—rather, the *proper* education—is vital to growth, expansion, leadership, success, confidence, and the future of your dreams. Make daily education a goal and give it the proper time, attention, and environment needed to absorb its precious and essential content.

 Reflect:

1. Name an activity, event, club, or society in which you are involved or would like to be involved. How did you decide this was right for you? What questions did you ask yourself when considering this decision?

2. Name three people who came to mind while considering what to choose. Why did they come to mind? What effect did they have on you? Was it favorable or unfavorable?

3. Why are extracurricular activities important to you? What are the right reasons to join? What are some wrong reasons to join? Have you ever joined for a "wrong" reason? If so, describe the situation. What would you change? What did you do right?

4. How important are academics to you? Why? Describe the effort you apply to your studies.

5. Where do you find your sources of research and information? How do you verify they are credible and truthful?

6. Where would you like your education to take you? Describe some of your goals, dreams, and a timeframe in which to reach them. What type of education is likely to get you there?

7. What obstacles are there in pursuing this type of education? Write down as many ideas for overcoming these obstacles as possible. Add to this list when new ideas come to mind.

CHAPTER 7

Obedience to Authority

Where Does Your Obedience Lie?

> *Control the manner in which a man interprets his world, and you have gone a long way toward controlling his behavior.*
> —Stanley Milgram

In 1961, psychologist Stanley Milgram began preparation for a series of social psychology experiments, known as the Milgram Experiment, measuring the willingness of men to obey an authority figure who *"instructed them to perform acts conflicting with their personal conscience."*[2] The basis of these experiments was obedience to authority figures. The experiments began a year after the trial of Adolph Eichmann in Jerusalem, with the intent of answering the question, *"Could it be that Eichmann and his million accomplices in the Holocaust were just following orders? Could we call them all accomplices?"*—Milgram 1974. Milgram was examining justifications for acts of genocide offered by those accused at the World War II Nuremberg War Criminal trials. The defense they used was based on the excuse of "obedience." They claimed they were "just following orders" from their superiors.

Participants in this experiment were led to believe they were assisting an unrelated experiment, in which they had to administer electric shocks, ranging from a mild initial shock of fifteen volts and extending to a four hundred and fifty volts of severe and dangerous shock, to a person in another room who was a student learning. The shocks were given with each incorrect answer the student provided, each one progressively more intense. In reality, this other person was an actor. Yet, the participant was led to believe that for each wrong answer, the student was to receive an electrical shock at variably increasing volts, including a level considered fatal. In reality, no such punishment actually occurred. Prerecorded blood-curdling sounds were prepared to add to the ambience of shock therapy.

It was found that a large percentage of participants would fully obey the instructions despite being uncomfortable. When the participant refused to administer a shock, the experimenter was to give a series of four orders to encourage and ensure they continued. They displayed varying degrees of tension and stress as a result, including sweating, trembling, stuttering, biting their lips, groaning, nervous laughing fits, seizures, and digging their fingernails. Every participant paused the experiment at least once to question it. After being assured by the experimenter, all participants continued with the experiment to three hundred volts, and two-thirds continued to the full four hundred fifty volts, which is a potentially fatal level.

Milgram summarized the experiment in his 1974 article *"The Perils of Obedience,"* writing, *"The legal and philosophical aspects of obedience are of enormous importance, but they say very little about how most people behave in concrete situations. I set up a simple experiment at Yale University to test how much pain an ordinary citizen would inflict on another person simply because he was ordered to by an experimental scientist. Stark authority was pitted against the subjects' strongest moral imperatives against hurting others, and, with the subjects' ears ringing with the screams of the victims, authority won more often than not. The extreme willingness of adults to go to almost any lengths on the command of an authority constitutes the chief finding of the study and the fact most urgently demanding explanation. Ordinary people, simply doing their jobs and without any particular hostility on their part, can become agents in a terrible destructive process. Moreover, even when the destructive effects of their work become patently clear, and they are asked to carry out actions incompatible with fundamental standards of morality, relatively few people have the resources needed to resist authority."*

STUDENTS: WHO CONNECTS YOUR DOTS?

Milgram was interested in discovering how far people would go regarding obeying an instruction, even at the cost of harming another person. There came the point where the participants no longer saw themselves as responsible for their actions and proceeded to evoke what they thought was harm onto another person. They became a vessel to carry out the instructions of another and submit to their authority, regardless of the consequences. For more information, online research will lead you to many summaries of this experiment and related links. Take some time to learn more about these experiments and the interpretations that resulted.

How do you see this happening in the world today? Can you see any examples in your life that replicate, or are a variation of, these types of actions? Could it be that people will just blindly follow authority, even at the risk of harming another person? What people in authority today have the opportunity to do this very same action? Have you ever been in this position, either as the one in authority or as the participant? How can you use CT skills to reason out a logical answer to this dilemma?

Thoughts about the Milgram Experiment:

1. *Personalization.* The students were not "personalized" to the participants. There is a lot to be said about human nature and personal relationships. When you know someone intimately, the close bond creates an emotional attachment, making it more difficult to consider any sense of harm.

    Whereas in the experiments, not knowing the students personally allowed the participants to disconnect from the emotional aspect of the experiment, excluding the morality conscience variable that was present. This variable could be overcome in the name of science and also via submission to the authority of the experimenter in charge. Do you think the results would have been different if a personal relationship existed between the participants and the students, or in this case, actors?

How would you have responded if you were a participant and you personally knew the student? What if the student was a family member or other loved one? What if you didn't know the student? What if you *were* the student? Would your relationship with the student bear any relevance on the decision you would make to, or not to, inflict harm on someone stemming from orders from an authority figure?

How about for a cause? How else might you be affected in your obedience to authority regarding issues of relationships with another? As the world becomes smaller and your freedoms continue to slip away, consider how you may be placed in a situation of obedience versus relationships. How would you respond if a similar occurrence happened in your class, work, a group, social, or organizational setting? Consider how you would handle this situation. What other CT questions would you ask regarding the relationship factor?

2. *Obedience for a cause.* Most of the participants, even if reluctant, continued to inflict what they believed to be painful electric shocks upon students because that is what they were told to do. At one point or another, each one requested confirmation for assurance they were doing the right thing and received it. Some were said to have proceeded in the name of science, believing they were responding to what they considered a "good cause."

How would you react in this scenario? If presented with the same situation, would you blindly follow orders because you were told to do so, knowing you were severely hurting a random person? Or would you blindly follow orders in the name of science or for some other good cause? Would you think critically about whether or not it would be okay to inflict harm upon another innocent person for any reason? Would you obey like a loyal dog given an order? Or would your innate sense of morality prevent you from inflicting pain?

Think of a scenario in your environment today where a cause of importance to you comes to mind. What are you willing to do for this cause? Would you allow harm to be inflicted upon someone else, whether the person is known personally or not, for the sake of the cause? Who would benefit from this occurring? Would you have a moral dilemma if the reason was "for a cause"? What factors would make this okay in your mind? What factors would cause it to be not okay? How would you be affected if you were put in this situation?

What if you were the one afflicted? How would you feel on the opposing side of the situation? Would your values come into play? How will you prepare for a similar situation to potentially affect you today? What other critical thoughts come to mind?

3. *Herd-mentality.* It has been said and is proven to be true that there is strength in numbers. As the participants observed their peers continuing to shock students despite the blood-curdling pain responses, they claimed they felt more justified as they were following suit. In society today, do you see evidence of this type of behavior? When more and more people come together, is there a growing strength and conviction in their actions and inhibitions?

Have you ever found yourself in a situation where you had a certain belief, but because of the crowd or group you were entangled with, you changed your choice and followed the crowd? What were the circumstances? How have you been influenced when the majority of people made it clear your choice or opinion was "wrong" and theirs was "right?" Did you stand your ground for what you believed in?

It is difficult to go against the grain. Think about how determined salmon are to swim against the current to migrate back to their origins. They are not influenced by the water current flowing in the opposite direction or any other neighboring creatures among them. Nothing can prevent them from doing what they know they must do.

What questions come to mind about how you react to differing crowds? What would happen if you stood your ground? Would you be willing to harm another person based on the influence of a crowd or group? Have you considered their intentions or what they are saying or thinking? Is there a "happy medium" between your viewpoint and theirs? Or deep down, do you still believe your original thought?

How can you assess the situation and verify that you align with your values? Your values are being challenged by an increasing rate (of alarm) daily. Identify your own moral code and belief system, and align your thoughts and actions with your values. How must you intensify your convictions so you are less likely to sway from them? How can you remain strong in your own decisions based on your individual values? What other critical questions can you ask to explore this common scenario further?

4. *Intimidation.* There is a right and a wrong expression of authority. Recall your own innate sense of right and wrong—your code of morality. Your conscience will guide you if something is not right. It is important to have order in society and to be obedient to the laws of the land. But how would you respond under intimidating circumstances? In the experiment, the participants were reassured they were to follow the experimenter. He was in authority, which is indirectly an element of intimidation.

What would result if the rules weren't followed? Would there be a penalty? Would they become one of the students and be subjected to shocks? What part of intimidation is responsible for how someone reacts? In a similar scenario, how would you be affected by intimidation? Would you react a certain way in anticipation of a negative result if you did not comply? What would happen if you obeyed, knowing there was an infliction of pain upon another person? What would happen to you if you disobeyed? Would you have a mental dilemma regarding your choices? How would the program be affected if you didn't obey?

Are you strong enough in society to choose what you consider right despite an intimidating outcome? How about despite intimidating pressure? What forms of intimidation reach and affect you? How do you respond to them? How can you overcome them? Think of a scenario today where you are being pressured in an intimidating manner. What are the circumstances? What are your options for responding? Will your values be compromised? What are your values? Are they clearly defined? Are you willing to fight for them? Are you secure with who you are and willing to stand up for your values despite intimidation? How will you know what to stand up for if your values are not defined? Prepare for how you would respond to intimidation in your current environment.

5. *Code of ethics.* Are you good with your word? Perhaps some of the participants continued because they committed themselves to the experiment. There was an ethical obligation to participate because they said they would. Do you do what you say and say what you do? What do you stand for? Who do you stand for? What can you think of that would cause you to back out of what you said you would do? Where do you draw the line? What is your own personal ethics code?

How would you respond if you committed to something and then realized later it violated your values somehow? What effects would this have on you? Where does your loyalty lie? How do your values affect the choices you make? Do you discover what a project or commitment entails before agreeing to pursue it? How can you prevent this situation from happening in the first place? What questions can you ask before you give your word or sign on the dotted line? Will you allow your values to be compromised?

6. *Location.* The setting may have been an influential factor in the experiment. Perhaps the industrial-like or professional lab-type setting affected the participants. How would a formal location affect people? How might a "softer" setting make any difference? How would the technical equipment affect the participants? What effect would the sight and thought of the shock machine have on them? How about the proximity to the students?

    How are you affected by location? Do you respond differently in a "sterile" environment than in a cozy, friendly environment? Would your values be defended differently in either case? What type of location would affect your decisions? Think about how you would respond to authority in your school or workplace versus a family setting. Would you compromise your values in any of them?

7. *The demeanor of the experimenter.* Perhaps the personality and demeanor of the one in charge swayed the degree of obedience. What effect could a certain personality have on the participants? What if the experimenter was gentle? What if the experimenter was brash and unapproachable? Would the personality have any effect at all?

    How do you handle situations when the one in authority has a distinct personality? How do you respond to a gentle persuasion? How about a "brazen" persuasion? What would you do differently in each situation?

    What if you discover the authority figure has a mentally challenged personality, such as narcissism? How would you respond knowing there is an embedded lack of concern or compassion for others? How is your performance affected by a shy leader? How about an aggressive leader? Have you ever let your values become compromised based on personality? How can you prepare yourself to do the "right" thing, in your eyes, no matter what personality you are dealing with?

8. *Settings.* Along with the location, perhaps the colors in the room affected the processing of information. Could the layout of the room and the chosen décor have affected the "personality" of the room? How could the temperature affect the participants? Was the temperature warm, cool, or comfortable? What other sounds could be heard? Were there any defining scents or odors that could have affected the participants? How would the sound of the blood-curdling screams affect them?

   How does a setting affect how you respond to authority? Would different settings change your responses in any way? How does temperature affect you? What if there were extreme temperatures? Would you be persuaded? How do lighting, colors, or smells affect your decision-making process? Would any of it affect your obedience to authority? Would compassion prevail over obedience? Or would obedience stand as the decision made to honor authority despite setting variations?

   Is there a factor regarding the degree of the screams or moans? Would the intensity cause differing responses? What other factors could be influential to you? How can you prepare yourself to stand firm in your own values without prejudice or influence?

How far are you willing to go for the sake of obedience? Where does your obedience lie? Or maybe, "how" does your obedience "lie"? Do you clearly delineate what is acceptable and what borders on wrong or immoral? When is it okay and actually appropriate to follow authority? When is it okay not to follow?

For the most part, it is important to be obedient to authority. However, when something occurs against your moral code, or you have this uneasy feeling or sense that something just isn't right, ask questions. Critically think about all aspects of the situation at hand and find out as much information as possible. Consider both sides of the story and weigh the possibilities. Do not blindly follow the crowd if you do not know where they are going or if you know something isn't as it should be. Be authentic. Stand by your innate sense of right and wrong, and critically think your way to a resolution you can live with. Be brave and endure the process, guided wisely by your defined values. It is wise to follow authority, yet do your own due diligence to ensure the authority is appropriate.

> *The disappearance of a sense of responsibility is the most far-reaching consequence of submission to authority.*
> —Stanley Milgram

> *It may be that we are puppets—puppets controlled by the strings of society. But at least we are puppets with perception, with awareness. And perhaps our awareness is the first step to our liberation.*
> —Stanley Milgram

> *It is not so much the kind of person a man is as the kind of situation in which he finds himself that determines how he will act.*
> —Stanley Milgram

> *The essence of obedience consists in the fact that a person comes to view himself as an instrument for carrying out another person's wishes, and he, therefore, no longer regards himself as responsible for his actions.*
> —Stanley Milgram

> *Each individual possesses a conscience that, to a greater or lesser degree, serves to restrain the unimpeded flow of impulses destructive to others. But when he merges his person into an organizational structure, a new creature replaces autonomous man, unhindered by the limitations of individual morality, freed of humane inhibition, mindful only of the sanctions of authority.*
> —Stanley Milgram

 **Reflect:**

1. What was the objective of the Milgram Experiments?
2. Read three different versions of the experiments and the summaries they provide. Write an essay about your interpretation of the findings.
3. How do you respond to appropriate authorities, such as parents, guardians, teachers, coaches, local law authorities, etc.?
4. How do you respond to authority when it is aligned with your values?
5. How do you respond to authority when it is not aligned with your values?
6. Think about a controversial issue regarding obedience. Ask yourself three unbiased questions from the point of view that you favor. Next, ask yourself three unbiased questions from the opposing point of view, and consider all responses objectively and with an open mind. What did you notice?
7. How would you respond if you were in a group and nine people thought one way, and you thought another? Would you alter your view or stand your ground? What if they put pressure on you? What if only you put pressure on you because you thought differently? What CT questions could you ask to assess the situation properly?
8. In a situation regarding obedience, how would you respond to volatile words like "outrage," "shocking," "urgent," etc.? Would you be intimidated to respond if someone was pressuring you? Ask yourself five CT questions the next time you feel someone is trying to manipulate you by intimidation.
9. How can you stand by your innate sense of right and wrong and remain obedient? Create a difficult scenario (verbally or in writing) involving authority you disagree with and describe how you would take appropriate actions to respond ethically.

CHAPTER 8

Social Media and Electronics

Tools or temptations?

At this point, it is almost hard to imagine life before social media. For some, there probably is no "before." It has likely become a staple in your daily life. How do you view social media? Which platforms are you involved in? Why did you choose them? Which ones aren't you involved with and why? Can you "take it or leave it?" How many times a day do you find the need to check the website or open the app? How often do you think about it?

Electronics have also become a staple in society, being found in the hands of three-year-olds through ninety-year-olds alike! Which electronics do you have? How did you choose them? How many are in your family? Which ones are used the most? What are they used for? How often do you use some type of electronic throughout the day? Is the amount of time you have access to the devices timed or limited? How do you utilize the devices?

Social media platforms and electronics can be used in many different ways. While some ways are positive, encouraging, helpful, and productive, others are negative and even destructive. Let's explore this further.

Reasons to use social media and electronics:

1. *To connect.* Using electronics with social media platforms is an excellent way to connect with friends, family, business

associates, etc. It's amazing how these items have brought people together and made the world a little smaller. Long-distance phone calls are virtually a thing of the past as phones, iPads, and computers have made it possible to connect and "Facetime" loved ones as if they were standing in the room with you at no additional cost. It is a means of reaching out and staying in touch in a simple and more complete manner.

2. *To find.* Not only do social media and electronics make it simple to connect with people, they also make it possible to find people. There was a time when you had to search phone directories or call the operator in the hopes of finding someone, often without complete access. Yet, if they were unlisted or moved around for various reasons, it was almost impossible to reach them. It is now possible to find people with little effort and probably discover more about them than you care to know! Even distant ancestries can be discovered and explored simply by tapping the keyboard and a search bar.

3. *To share information.* Using electronics to access various platforms, there are innumerable ways of sharing information at the touch of a keystroke or tap of a screen. Pictures, documents, recipes, maps, locations, etc., can be shared within fractions of a second. Apps even allow people to share information within a defined group with a common cause, such as teams within a school or organization, saving time from individual messages and reaching everyone simultaneously. You are able to upload, download, and scan to your heart's content.

4. *To market or advertise.* Let's face it: sometimes, you just can't take the business mindset out of the person. Electronic devices and social media platforms are prime opportunities to promote products, services, or events and build a business. There are many apps, groups, and platforms for bartering, buying, and selling, as well as promoting business services or opportunities. Increasingly, online businesses are taking

over for brick-and-mortar status ones, making social media and the use of electronics absolutely essential for business success. Access is now available through electronic devices and social media to reach the entire world in just seconds.

5. *For entertainment.* Many forms of entertainment are found through either social media or electronic devices. Streaming shows, videos, or playing games are all possible through this means. There is solo entertainment or even group involvement opportunities. There is literally every topic available to spark the interest of everyone and anyone willing to engage.

6. *For education.* Online schools are here to stay and have a place for certain diligent and self-motivating students. Many regular schools also offer an online option through their main campus, and homeschooling has reached its highest popularity status. The content itself is also accessible by virtually every available cyber means. It is possible to look up calculators, spelling, definitions, courses, descriptions, and how-to instructional videos. Almost anything can be discovered, learned, or "self-taught." Many brick-and-mortar schools are now foregoing textbooks for an online curriculum, where electronics are a must. Knowledge of virtually anything is literally at your fingertips.

7. *For work.* Work utilizes many of the different reasons already mentioned. For example, an author may spend the better part of the day using electronics to write a manuscript in preparation for print. A pharmacist, nurse, or doctor may access patient databases on electronics to review a medical history. An attorney or paralegal may delve into hours of previous case research for an upcoming trial. A business owner may research the web to discover which audience to focus a new campaign on. A firefighter or police officer may rely on a GPS to get him or her quickly to the scene of an accident. Technology has completely changed the way careers are performed.

STUDENTS: WHO CONNECTS YOUR DOTS?

How do you use social media and electronics? Who do you connect with? Do you connect with the right people? How do you determine who you connect with? Do you know everyone you connect with? What is the connection between you and them? What is the reason for the connection? Are they family members or close friends? Is there anyone you are connected with that you aren't comfortable with? How did they get on your list? Do you feel safe with each of your connections? Are you able to remove them from your access if you feel uncomfortable with the connection?

Is there a connection with someone you want to hide from others? Or can you be transparent with all of them? It is important to connect with the "right" people. Always know who is on your list and have them there for a legitimate purpose. Be able to share your list with anyone, meaning be particular about whom you communicate with and build a connection. Who is trying to connect with you? Will you give them access? What if you do not know them? As access to other people becomes easier and easier, critically think about your situation and who you are comfortable being in contact with. Would your parents or guardians approve? Would your friends or other people close to you approve? Think logically about each decision you make.

Do you have a "need" for "likes" on social media? If so, why do you think that is? Do your mood or "feelings" change based on the number of likes from a post? Do you feel this is a healthy response to base your feelings on? What would be a more sincere thing to base emotions on? Do you feel secure enough in yourself? Are you confident in your own qualities or characteristics? How can you become less dependent on likes? Begin to think critically and use logic.

Do you use social media and electronics to find people? Are they people you should be looking for? Are you careful in your searches? Is there a legitimate purpose for searching for particular people? Do you have anything to hide about your searches? What are your intentions for searching? Ensure your intentions are good and you are being safe and appropriate with each search you perform. Some people have become so good at hiding their identity, hacking into accounts, and being deceitful in who they really are and their intentions. Know this as you spend time in the unknown cyber world. Not everyone has good intentions for you, and you must always take extra precautions to protect yourself. Be careful about who you are searching for and how you are searching for them.

Social media and electronics are excellent means for sharing a wide variety of things. Pictures can be shared via Dropbox, Google Drive, and AirDrop applications. Virtually all social apps allow for storylines, photos, and even interactive methods of sharing all sorts of information. What types of things do you share? What is shared with you? Has the content in either case ever been questionable? Can everything be shown to parents, guardians, teachers, or other friends? Have you ever considered listening to something questionable? What do you consider questionable? How does this align with your values?

Once information is out on the web, it is possible that it could be around *forever*. Are you willing to take that risk with sensitive information? You may have heard of cases where people felt uninhibited and shared some very personal things, such as pictures or private information, only to have them exposed for the world to see, causing irreparable damage for years or even decades to come. What would cause people to share such private information? Do you ever feel forced to share things you aren't comfortable sharing? Is there anything that would make you feel obligated? How much control do you believe you have over your content? Is it kept securely? Does anyone else have access to it? Do you protect yourself? With cameras in all the smartphones and tablets, have you ever thought about information, or even images, being recorded of you without your knowledge? Learn to avoid vulnerable situations and maybe even cover the cameras while changing or showering—*just in case*. Be aware of what others around you are doing with their devices as well.

Have you ever sold or bought anything online or through social media on an electronic device? What was the experience like? Did you advertise or use the media for marketing products or services? Have you read or watched the content of other people's advertisements? Do you have your devices set to block inappropriate content? There are some bad people out there who thrive on corrupting others, and they do so in the form of temptation. They may try to advertise or promote something they feel they can persuade you with. By reducing the likelihood of temptation in the first place, such as by activating blocks on your devices, you protect yourself against unnecessary obstacles. The blocks aren't always foolproof, so still be cautious about the content that comes through your devices. While it is easy to believe you can overlook all attempts, temptations are just that—*tempting!* Prevention is the absolute key to avoidance.

In 2013, the President of the United States signed the Smith-Mundt Modernization Act of 2012 (2012 – H.R. 5736), allowing the propagation of "disinformation" or misinformation by the media. In other words, the media in all forms have been permitted to manipulate, persuade, and deceive people through propaganda with the intent of influencing people to their product or viewpoint. This fact alone should be reason enough to motivate you to always think critically about media content.

If media content, including major news outlets, social media, journalism, TV, etc., is not required to be truthful, what do you suppose the reason is for "censoring" or "canceling" certain people or their content? It isn't because of inaccurate or misinformation, as often stated, as it has been permitted and encouraged since the act was signed in 2013. Do you realize the ones *doing* the censoring or canceling are *afraid* of what you might find out? They do not want you to know what someone else has to share. They want to hide this information. What are they afraid of? People have a right to freedom of speech, so is it right to prevent anyone from this freedom? Who is doing something wrong in this case? Whenever you recognize censoring or canceling occurring, think critically about the message or person being censored or banned somehow. They have obviously discovered something of interest. Do extra research with an open mind and consider what they try to share. Find more unbiased information and analyze the data in their message. Then, do research and find out more information about the one doing the censoring and objectively unveil the reason for their fear and insecurity. Find out as much information as possible about *both* sides using unbiased data and drawing your own conclusion.

Entertainment is a predominant reason for the use of electronics. Have you ever played a game on a device? Or, more accurately, —

which ones—have you played? Do you play simple games to pass the time while waiting, such as solitaire, word games, or even Candy Crush? Or are you an intense "gamer" indulging in large monitors, fancy controllers, and stimulating action?

How much of your time is spent on gaming? Are you able to walk away at any time? What is your favorite game, and why? Do you play educational games? Do you allow games to take you away from reality for a while? What is your ultimate goal in gaming? Do you play by yourself or with others? Are your choices of games transparent? Do they align with your values? Is there anything embarrassing about your selection? Do you ever hide what you are doing? What portion of your day involves gaming? Have you ever felt you were unable to walk away from gameplay? How often do you think about playing?

How about other sources of entertainment, such as streaming movies or shows? How often do you do this? What about YouTube or other videos? What content do you seek? Do you listen to music online? What music do you choose to listen to? Are you selective and align the choices with your values? Are they artists or songs you can share with your parents or guardians? What is your main goal with the selected content? Is it usually informative, educational, or for pure entertainment? Do you recognize the creators of some games and other entertainment may not have your best interests and safety in mind? Can you identify temptation or attempts at temptation? Are you secure enough to avoid compromising content?

Do you ever choose electronic viewing over spending time with another person? Do you put devices in front of people? Do you feel more comfortable texting someone rather than speaking to them in person? If so, why do you think that is? Do you feel it is a problem in need of attention? What changes might need to be made? Who can you share this with who will positively support you?

How much time do you spend on social media for entertainment? What part do you find entertaining? Which applications do you use? Why do you find this entertaining? What else do you do for entertainment?

What portion of your education involves electronic devices? Do you work digitally at school or utilize textbooks? How often do you search outside of schoolwork for educational purposes? What information do you generally seek? Is it for do-it-yourself purposes or to gain additional knowledge in general? Is your research for legitimate purposes? Are you able to share your findings with others? How much time do you spend on educational learning or research? Do you question the sources? How do you know if the sources you are using are credible? How might you find out this information? How can you determine if there is misinformation? How do you sort through the advertisements and propaganda? How can you verify the content? Learn to recognize when there is a political message attached to education. Education is supposed to be about gaining knowledge, learning how to do something, or how something works. It should *never* involve any type of sociopolitical message intertwined.

Are you currently working? How much time does your work demand for you to be on an electronic device or social media? Do you work off of a laptop or desktop? Do you use an iPad or iPhone for business matters? What happens if the internet is down? Could your projects survive without the use of devices? Do you have pop-ups blocked?

There is a time and place for electronic devices and social media as well. It is becoming increasingly difficult to navigate your day without using electronics in one form or another. As schools, jobs, and even communication become more reliant on electronics, there is a need to take precautions to guard against unwarranted propaganda, temptations, and distractions these devices can depict. In what ways can you be proactive to avoid these things? It is also important to be able to walk away from these devices when there is no need for them. Give your hands, posture, eyes, and mind the desperately needed electronic freedom.

 Reflect:

1. How many electronic devices do you have? How many are in your home? How often are each of them used? How often are they updated or replaced?

2. How many social media platforms are you signed up for? How many are you actively involved with? What is your primary purpose for each one? How often do you access each of them daily?

3. Is it important to count how many "likes" you receive when you post an image or commentary? How much emphasis do you place on the responses you receive? Do you feel your self-worth is tied to social media? What are positive things to attach to your self-worth? What are ways you can build up your self-worth? What types of things could tear it down?

4. Discuss how you use social media/electronics to connect with people. Discuss how you use them to find people. Discuss what types of things you share on social media/electronics. Discuss whether you have ever used social media/electronics for marketing or propaganda. Discuss how you use social media/electronics for entertainment. Discuss how social media and electronics can be used for educational or work purposes.

5. How can electronics and social media be used negatively? Name as many ways as you can think of. Have you ever chosen to use them in any of these ways? What were the reasons?

6. How can you protect yourself from unwarranted content on your devices? What would you do if a friend began to lead you down a negative path you knew was wrong? How can you remain confident and secure enough to make good choices?

7. How can you implement CT methods to help you make good decisions? Have you previously used CT when making choices regarding electronic devices and social media? What are some questions you could ask?

8. The decisions and choices you make today can have a lifelong impact. Name some ways making bad decisions today could negatively impact your future using these devices and platforms.

9. Compare how much time you spent with friends face-to-face this week versus via electronic devices. What do you notice?

10. How much time do you think is too much time on devices? What is your reasoning? Discuss how you reached your answer. Have you ever wondered if you were addicted to gaming, electronics, or social media? Where would you go for help if you did? What are the signs of addiction to each of these things?
11. How can your health be affected by the overuse of electronic devices? Explain.

CHAPTER 9

Peer Pressure

What do you know about peer pressure? Is it knowledge from what you have heard and read? Or is it from *actual* experience? How would you define peer pressure in your terms? In what ways does it affect you today? How did it affect you in the past? Do you anticipate any issues in the future? In what ways?

No one is immune to peer pressure. It occurs from your earliest memories, perhaps in kindergarten or even preschool, and continues throughout your lifetime. In general, it is pressure from others to do something that is usually unlawful, uncomfortable, disobedient, immoral, unhealthy, risky, or premature. There are various categories of peer pressure. Some of them include pressure to steal, cheat, hurt someone, lie, smoke, take unprescribed drugs, be intimate outside of marriage, gamble, or do something else you aren't ready to do, such as jump out of an airplane or some other risky act. What other common things can you think of that involve peer pressure?

Think of some actual experiences when you felt pressured by someone else. Have they been recently? How did you handle them? Would you change any of your actions or inactions? What do you think you did correctly? Who was involved? Were the issues resolved? What did you learn from the experiences? What insights are you able to share with others?

Generally, when you think of "peer" pressure, you think of someone with a similar status, such as a student, sibling, or friend. This section will include "peer" pressure as any pressure applied to you in an unethical, unwarranted, or inappropriate manner, including those in authority over you and those younger or under you. Essentially, we will discuss any type of unnecessary pressure causing you to feel influenced to act or not act in a certain way.

Now that you have identified who can cause peer pressure and discussed situations involving the pressure, let's focus on how to handle these circumstances. Consider how you responded during times of pressure. What felt right regarding how you handled it? What did you feel unsure of or would like help with?

Ways to handle peer pressure:

1. *Tell someone.* There is almost always someone *not* involved in the situation who can objectively and trustingly view what you are experiencing. In medicine, a well-known saying is, *"If you see something, say something."* Don't be afraid to involve someone else in what you are experiencing. If you aren't sure if something is okay or if you feel uncomfortably pressured, run it by someone you trust.

    Sometimes, the act of talking aloud allows you to see things from a different perspective or simply clarifies the situation. When you think about it *and* hear the words out loud, a different part of your brain begins to process the situation as well. You will begin to formulate new ideas in your mind, plus reap the benefits of the thoughts of a trusted friend or family member with your best interests at heart.

    Who can you think of that you could trust personal information with? How many people who love you and would help you work through a difficult or compromising situation where you feel pressured come to mind? Take some time to formulate a list, even if it's just in your mind, of people you can trust if you feel pressured in some way. Be open to many possibilities, including family, friends, neighbors, teachers, coaches, pastors, and others. Knowing in advance you have the support of others builds confidence in being strong in your convictions.

2. *Remove yourself from the situation.* If you are safely able, remove yourself from the uncomfortable situation. For example, if you innocently bought tickets for a movie that appeared to be worthwhile, yet while watching it, it became compromising, be strong and independent enough to get up and walk away. Or if you were trying to watch calories to fit into a tux or gown for homecoming, but someone was trying to entice you with the sights and smells of a bakery, walk away and remove yourself from the temptation.

Temptations can be big or small, and the pressure from others can also be big or small. It doesn't have to be just something morally compromising. The pressure could go against a conviction you made to yourself or others. Or simply personal goals you are trying to achieve.

Have you ever been in a situation that suddenly became uncomfortable with pressure? If so, how did you handle it? Were you able to physically walk away? Were you strong enough mentally to walk away? Describe the situation. Who was involved? How was the pressure applied? What do you think you did well? What would you change?

If you haven't been in a pressured situation, how do you think you would handle it? Do you feel strong enough to do what is right despite pressure? Would the type of pressure that was applied matter? Would it matter who applied the pressure? What are some ideas you could think of about how to prepare for an encounter like this? Be willing to safely remove yourself from the situation if possible.

3. *Call out for help.* If circumstances elevate, call out for help or cause loud noises so you can be heard. It is possible a situation may occur where you feel you could use the help and support of others. Don't be afraid to yell for help or even make as loud of a distraction as you can to get someone else's attention. Consider having a whistle on your

person—in your book bag, pocket, or purse. You can't go wrong by being prepared. Any loud sound may be enough to send the pursuer full speed ahead away from you.

Perhaps it is simply a matter of placing an actual call for help. Do you have a phone you keep with you? Do you have easy access to the phone numbers of people who can help you quickly? Create a favorites list of people for quick access.

Have you ever been in a situation where you called, whistled, or created a distraction for help? Describe the circumstance. How did the sounds affect the situation? What other ways can you think of that would cause a distraction? How can you be prepared to call for help in different situations? Discuss the possibilities.

4. *Just say no.* Be level-headed and lean on the morals you uphold. Stand your ground and do not let anyone persuade you against what you know is right. Be willing and able to say "no" if you are pressured to do, say, see, or intake anything you know contradicts laws, rules, your health, or your values.

You have a bright future in front of you. One wrong decision could change your promising course forever. Sometimes, all it takes to prevail and stay on course is one simple word—no. It is a powerful word that is courageous and shows the strength of character when used to uphold your principles. You will gain more respect by standing your ground with a confident "no" than by weakly conforming to the persuasion and insecurity of others trying to lower you to their level.

Has there ever been a time when you were presented with something against your morals, and you responded with a firm "no"? Or perhaps a friendly "no, thank you"? Or maybe it was a passionate "NO!" Was it easy for you to say? Or are you easily influenced by others, especially if they show aggressiveness in their actions? How can you prepare yourself to say no readily when in a compromising situation awaiting your response?

5. *Avoid pressured situations.* If you know in advance someone may try to pressure you to do something you know is wrong or uncomfortable, do your best to avoid the situation to begin with. Avoidance is always the key to preventing an unwarranted interaction involving pressure.

    Find a new route to travel or join a different club if possible. It may not always be easy to accept your second choice as your selection, but it may be worth it if this leads to a safer circumstance and avoids a pressured situation. You may also learn new things along the way or find other opportunities in the process. For example, a fitness center with the best and latest equipment may also have a reputation for "riff-raff" trying to sell illegal products. The best idea is to avoid this club entirely and find one closer to home, school, or work, or maybe even come across one with a new sauna or a friendlier staff. Be open to exploring new opportunities or services in a safer and unpressured atmosphere.

    If a friend wants to go to a movie that you know violates your principles or to a party that will be loud, unmonitored, and most likely illegal, avoid the situation in the first place, however it seems fit. Make alternate plans to be busy during that time, suggest other things to do, or avoid the situation by simply saying no.

    What are other ways you can think of to avoid pressured situations? Have you ever been in a situation where applying any of these options was necessary? Describe the circumstances involved. If you know about them in advance, are you strong enough to avoid pressured situations? What is your preferred method of avoidance?

6. *Pair-up.* There is strength in numbers. Stick close to your friends, family, and even an agreed-upon accountability partner. If you are selective in choosing your friends, you

will develop life-long, unbreakable friendships. Be sure in advance they share your values and morals. It is important to be matched up with like-minded people who will support you and what you stand for and believe in.

Whether a close friend or family member, be committed to making good choices and decisions and know that those who love you will stick with you through good times and bad. It is often easier to make the right decisions, especially if they are difficult ones, knowing you are accountable for your actions and report to someone else. For example, if you designate a friend to be your workout accountability partner and are committed to a set regimen you designed, but a group of other friends want to pressure you to go out for ice cream instead, know you can depend on your accountability partner to hold you to your commitment. Perhaps a competition is coming up, and you only have two more weeks to train. You have the support of your true friends and family to hold you to your commitment and love you enough to encourage you to do what's best for you right now. In this case, the pressure is not for something dangerous, but it is something that is currently working against the goals you set for yourself.

Temptation is most likely to occur when you are by yourself. Generally alone, you are most vulnerable and easily persuaded. Consider Jesus by Himself in the desert for forty days after He was baptized. The devil tempted Him with food and even false "power" if He gave in to the alluring temptations presented to Him. He resisted them all while focusing on what He set out to do.

In what ways have you been tempted in the past? Did you give in to the temptations? What were the surrounding circumstances? Was there anyone else involved to support you in making a good decision? What did you do right? What would you change if you could? Is there anything currently tempting you negatively? Who do you have in your support system? Who else can you think of to "pair up" with to strengthen you to make good choices?

Who do you help as an accountability partner? Are there other people you can pair up with to help strengthen or support through challenging times, especially involving decisions? What other scenarios can you think of where having the support of others would be helpful? Discuss these scenarios and how a partner could help you through them.

7. *Find or create a distraction.* Perhaps you find yourself drawn to or are presented with something wrong or immoral. Schedule something during that time or be around other people who can replace your thoughts or intentions. Busy yourself in a more productive or creative way.

Perhaps a group of friends is going to a party you already know in advance will be bad news. Ask another friend to go to a new local Escape Room, burger joint, or recreation park to shoot a few hoops. Many fun options are free or may cost a small fee to participate in. Run a few errands you have been putting off or visit some relatives you haven't seen for a while. Volunteer at a long-term care facility where residents would love a companion to talk to. Many possibilities exist to reframe your mind from what you know will have a negative outcome to something productive, favorable, rewarding, and even fun.

Have you experienced a time when you knew of a negative event happening you would be pressured to attend? What was the event? How did you handle the situation? Do you have any regrets? What alternatives did you sift through? What did you do that you are proud of? What would you change if you could? How will you handle future similar situations? Is there currently anything similar you are experiencing? Have a list of fun and interesting things to do rather than participate in anything that goes against your values.

8. *Preprogram your mind.* When you take time to "preprogram" your mind on how to handle yourself in various situations, your responses are automatic, and you will know how to handle yourself when the time arises. Preprogramming your mind takes thought and a conscious effort to identify and recognize a situation as needing preparation for automatic responses. Compare it to actions of a habit. When you are in the habit of doing something, it becomes so second nature that you do not have to think about how it will be done.

    Preprogram your mind to make decisions that align with your belief system and values. It is important to have already defined what your beliefs and values are. Define your beliefs. Define your values. Describe the type of person you are by defining ten of your character qualities. What lines will you not cross? Are there any that you will? What is important to you? How did you decide this? What other ways would you describe or define your beliefs or values?

    Now, match up your responses with your beliefs and values. Each time a decision is to be made, align it with your belief and value system, ensuring you do not cross the line. Think about various scenarios of pressured situations and your options for making decisions. Which ones align with your values? Which ones do not? Is it easier to make decisions when you have clearly defined values that define you?

    It is possible that in order to *preprogram* your mind, you might first need to *reprogram* your mind. Previously, have you made choices that violate your code of ethics? Have you ever made a knee-jerk reaction that went against your values and regretted it later? Sometimes, there is a need to recognize and reframe the current programming of your mind. It may take some time to declutter the previous and haphazard way of thinking and make way for new, improved thinking that aligns with your belief system.

    All the decisions you make are based on thoughts that you think. They are *all* a choice. You choose the thoughts and the way that you think. Knowing this, it is within your ability to declutter the bad thoughts, habits, and decision-making ability and replace and then reprogram your mind with a "preprogram" to instinctively revert to a way of thinking and making decisions that are aligned with your values. Making the right choice or decision will be a habit, even while under pressure.

Have you ever been presented with an immoral dilemma and found difficulty in making a decision? Using the values, beliefs, and character qualities you defined previously, what was the right decision to make? Was this decision more evident, having defined who you are and what you believe in? Be courageous and stand strong in your beliefs and ethical code. How can preprogramming your mind to align with your values and beliefs benefit you in future pressured situations? What steps will you take to *reprogram* your mind to the ideal *preprogram*?

9. *Think critically.* By thinking critically in every situation you encounter, you will be able to make logical decisions based on common sense and sound reasoning. Ask all of the CT questions as applicable, as defined in Chapter 1. A reminder follows:

CT Questions for Decision-Making:

1. What is the situation?
2. Who is involved?
3. What are your options?
4. Who will be affected by your decision?
5. How will you or they be affected by your decision?
6. Could anyone get hurt in the process?
7. Will your decision be something you can be proud of?
8. How will the decision shape your reputation or future?
9. How will the decision grow you as a person?

10. What are the potential consequences for each decision option available?
11. What is the right thing to do?
12. What obstacles might be clouding your judgment?
13. What option will lead to the best possible outcome?
14. What decision will be best for your legacy?
15. How did you reach your final decision?

Peer pressure, or pressure from any other person that makes you feel uncomfortable or like they violated your ethics, beliefs, or values, must be processed and appropriately addressed. Know the difference between the love and guidance of a parent or guardian pressing you to complete chores or go to a sibling's recital versus someone pressuring you to violate a law or value.

This chapter outlines nine methods of handling pressured situations. Memorize and preprogram them into your mind so they instinctively surface when in a pressured situation. Form a habit of your favorite methods and eliminate the uncertainty of pressured decision-making by automatically choosing the best response method. Let yourself become known as a force to be reckoned with, as one who consistently aligns with the values you define for yourself. Be consistent with who you say you are.

Be strong enough to stand alone, smart enough to know when you need help, and brave enough to ask for it.
—Ziad K. Abdelnour

Don't let the fear of standing alone prevent you from standing up for what is right.
—Jill Fandrich

 Reflect:

1. Name five different types of pressured situations. How would you handle each of them?
2. Have you ever encountered pressured situations? Describe them. How did you handle them? What did you do correctly? What would you do differently?
3. What are the nine ways mentioned to handle peer pressure? What other ways can you think of? Which way or ways come most easily to you?
4. Create a list of people you feel comfortable discussing pressured situations with. Are there any people that come to mind you would not discuss this with? Why?
5. How can you better prepare yourself to handle any future pressured situations? How can you prepare yourself for pressure in the workplace?
6. How can you prepare yourself to help other people in pressured situations?
7. Where can you find more information about handling pressured situations? How can you verify credible sources?

CHAPTER 10

Why Identify?

This chapter is designed to apply CT methods regarding the desire to have a label to "identify" placed on yourself, whatever that label may be. In today's society, some people have become enraptured with labeling themselves with one aspect of their being. Why has it become so important to pick out one of many attributes and tag yourself with it? Everyone is beautifully and wonderfully made. We have talents, ambitions, gifts, and magnificent abilities. Why is there a "strong desire" to overlook a multitude of endearing, and even impressive, qualities just to focus on a decision to think a particular thought and label oneself with this "identity"? More importantly, how did this become a movement and take flight to the point that our very own government now finds it necessary to create mandates regarding this desire to highlight one aspect in people?

How did you respond when you were younger and asked what you wanted to be "when you grew up"? Did you respond, "I want to be known and make my mark on this world, not for my talents, abilities, or character, but because I chose to have a certain type of preference"? Or did you have more talent-driven ambitions, such as to be an engineer or an athlete? Or maybe a firefighter or a doctor? Or perhaps a baker, geologist, or business owner of your own makings? At what point was the decision made to choose your "identity" based on one thought or preference?

How has society capitalized on the concept of defining yourself based on a thought or preference? How is it that some students have now lost their privacy in public school bathrooms? Some businesses now even require continuing education or required competencies to occur and be stored in personnel files for documentation regarding preference training. What about focusing on the safety of children? Or the security of our country? Could infrastructure be an important thing to focus on instead? How about the importance of a standard of conduct in companies, so employees are treated decently and are acknowledged for hard work and talent? How about analyzing companies' termination policies? How are businesses forced to become more concerned about a thought or "preference" rather than if someone is skillfully qualified to perform their job description? How did this happen? You are of more value than labeling yourself based on one thought of how you prefer something. More importantly, what can be done to refocus on priorities, and what would be the most efficient and productive manner of operation? Certainly, there must be a way that everyone can still be their own individual, yet not feel a need to define themselves by a single element and then force their preferences into mandates, changing school environments and how businesses operate. Why is there an increasing need to "identify" in any way in the first place?

Employees and employers are essentially forced to *favor* people with a different thought or "preference." What does that have to do with work? What is the basis of how this relates to work productivity and successful accomplishment? Have you noticed this in a school environment? What about innocent children who should focus on a playful childhood rather than focusing on "preferences"? This pressure has nothing to do with the child. It has everything to do with adults forcing the idea upon them. What is the reason for manipulating children, whose minds are not fully developed, to "identify" themselves in the first place? As a matter of fact, on average, the brain is not fully developed until approximately age twenty-five. Is it even logical to ignore this fact?

Why should public schools focus on how a person "identifies" rather than their educational needs? What does the public school system, and even some private ones, have to do with a focused look at a preference? For example, it is contradictory to have certain harassment policies in place yet force everyone to focus on their "sexual identity" and give special consideration to people who choose to make that the focus of their being rather than on education and building character.

What is the basis, or logic, for this focus? Where does it ultimately stem from? Why is society laying down a red carpet to oblige a need to label someone with an "identity"? Speaking from a CT point-of-view, it defies logic.

Potential reasons someone might feel a need to define themselves with a type of "identity":

1. *Insecurity.* Everyone has had some form of insecurity in their lives. It is part of human nature. An insecurity could dampen self-worth and cause someone to feel a need to define themselves in hopes of discovering a sense of security, even if it is a fabricated one. What insecurity comes to your mind that you endured yet overcame? Was it a long process? How did you overcome this obstacle? Did you use reason and logic to make sense of it?

   Are there any insecurities you can think of that still linger? How does a sense of insecurity present itself to you? How do you respond when you are made aware of an insecurity? Who or what is a potential source of insecurity to you? Is it generally from spoken words or an event that may or may not have happened?

   What are ways to try to work through insecurities and bring them to a resolution? Have you ever looked at the opposing side of an insecurity, if there is one? How could seeing an alternate version affect your perspective? What type of research did you perform to understand the source of the problem? How can you research authentically and factually while showing no emotional bias? Did you resolve the insecurity within your own means?

   Could there be an underlying insecurity causing the desire to express to the world a particular way to define yourself? What are the talents and abilities that you have been blessed with? How are you utilizing these skills productively in your life? What if you defined yourself based on a different aspect? How many attributes can you think of to define yourself? What would change if you chose a different one? What if you placed all definitions aside and allowed yourself to be considered a worthy individual who is good just as you are, without a label?

Discover the source of the insecurity using reason and logic. Make an intentional effort to uncover the source, and use skills and any necessary help to work through and heal the insecurity, leaving you better able to enjoy a content and fulfilled life.

2. *Herd-mentality.* Many things are easier when you are in the comfort and security of a group. As mentioned earlier, there is strength in numbers. Often, a combined sharing of different perspectives leads to productive solutions. As many come together with the same "desire" to feel accepted, building strength in almost anything becomes easier. Is the idea of acceptance from like-minded people causing more people to join a "bandwagon"? Is there comfort or a feeling of acceptance if you join in and align with others? Have you taken time to think about why this has happened? Is there a sense of obligation while in the presence of the group? Are you permitted to think critically for yourself and reach your own conclusions without fear of reprisal of some sort?

Sometimes, in a group setting, people can slip into a follower role, losing their true identity as individuals. Do you allow others to think for themselves without prejudice, respecting potentially different views? Are you able to still be yourself, despite potential persuasion, due to a group mentality? Are you highlighting your best characteristics? What are some of your other characteristics? Or are you just following a crowd? Do you find security under the umbrella of a group? What do you see as the benefit derived from a group? Would there be a bigger benefit from being away from the influence of the group? How would this be different? What factors have you considered in reaching your conclusion? Is there a chance you have given up your individual freedom for conformity?

3. *The desire for attention.* It can be difficult to always be in the background. Or to be shy and feel like you are unnoticed. Everyone appreciates at least a little attention at some point. Perhaps the desire to be seen and recognized for something is a reason for taking a defined outlook on life. Do you want to be noticed by people and catch their attention? Who would you like to be noticed by? Have you thought about different ways to reach people that might be captivating?

    In what ways have you tried to get involved? What other ways can you reach out and be noticed based on abilities or accomplishments? What would be the benefit of this? How are you impacted when you are noticed? How about when you are overlooked? Is this the best decision you reached regarding gaining some form of attention? What other forms of attention might be endearing? What may have happened in your past that led you to be subdued? What type of research might support the idea of drawing attention to yourself? Does defining yourself by choosing an "identity" satisfy your desire? If so, in what ways does this further your goals or values? What other attributes, characteristics, or actions might there be for being noticed? What type of attention might win people's hearts without biasing others?

4. *Peer pressure.* Peer pressure is a powerful force everyone has probably experienced at one point or another in their lives. While it could be a positive or negative force, it is generally considered negative, as it implies your ability, or opportunity, to control your own decisions are actually influenced and controlled by someone else. Are you being pressured to act in a certain way? Who might be putting unwarranted pressure on you? What would be the basis of this

pressure be? Who would benefit from following suit with this pressure? Do you pressure yourself to act or be a certain way? Has someone allowed you to feel the need to take a stand and narrow how you see yourself?

Was there a time in your life when you clearly felt pressured by your peers? What were the surrounding circumstances? How did you respond to this situation? What are other ways you could have responded to the situation? Were you able to remain strong and not allow yourself to be persuaded by others? What other thoughts do you have about peer pressure? Learn to recognize if someone attempts to snatch your power away from you by pressuring you to think or act like them. Be aware at all times of the possibility of someone, or something, trying to take control of your freedom and individuality. It can happen in the subtlest of ways.

Make an effort to see the situation from an opposing perspective, then evaluate your information in an unbiased manner. Question and discover more about the motives or agendas of others in persuasive situations. Ask yourself who benefits by giving up your control. Then, draw your own independent conclusion without pressure from others.

5. *Emotionally charged.* It can be very difficult to think straight when those around you are emotionally charged. It may even be a little, or a lot, intimidating! How about the way you make decisions when your emotions are running on the high side? How do you calm down and critically think about the situation? Has a highly emotional state, either yours or someone else's, been the driving force in feeling the desire to label yourself?

Emotions can be powerful yet may cloud the ability to think rationally. Getting caught up in an emotionally-driven cause or event is not hard. The influence can be formidable, as emotion may lead to unpredictability. What is the basis for your decision-making choices? How do emotions typically affect you? Can you think of a time when emotions clouded your decisions? What were the results of the situation? Who was involved and benefitted from the emotional stance?

How about a time when you overcame an emotional situation by resolving it rationally? What steps did you take for this to occur? Are there other areas of your life driven by emotions? How do you evaluate and handle emotional situations? What is your particular way to unwind or cope when emotions are involved? What is your source of replenishing calmness in your immediate environment? How can you gain more control over your emotions?

6. *Hurt.* We have all been hurt in one way or another in our lifetimes. No one leaves this world unscathed. It is probably almost guaranteed that we will be hurt again. The way pain is afflicted is different for every person. Yet, not everyone feels the need to react publicly. Some call it oppression and seek revenge. Others focus on healing themselves and building stronger, empowering, and uplifting qualities within themselves, transforming their negative energy into positive vibrations and pouring it out toward successful personal or professional development.

How do you handle mentally painful situations that occurred through no fault of your own? How about physically painful situations? How about a hurtful situation you may have caused, even if it was by accident? Do you let a historically painful event, unexperienced by you personally, control you and how you respond today? Do you let the pain define who you are and how you act or react? How would lashing out solve anything? Who benefits from being reactive rather than proactive? Do you understand that everyone has had some form of pain in their lives, not simply you?

While it is very unfortunate you are hurting, what are better methods to heal and remove the pain and move forward peacefully rather than allow yourself to be controlled by it? A choice can be made to find the source of the pain, address it in a healthy, positive, and beneficial way, and actually alleviate the hurt permanently! Have you taken the time to see things from an opposing perspective? Do you choose to be influenced by the pressure of others, or are you unwilling to act based on emotion and pressure?

How do you evaluate the source of the hurt? What methods do you undergo to heal? How can you alter any negative responses regarding the source of the pain? What do you know about the source of the pain? Who or what is the cause? What is your desired outcome of choosing an "identity" derived from a hurt? Does this permanently resolve the problem without harming or focusing on anyone else in the process, allowing contentment and productivity to prevail? What outcome do you extrapolate from a certain tag? Are you able to let go of bitterness and forgive? Or do you hold on to the bitterness, let it control you, and use it to inflame someone else? In what ways can you choose to let go of the hurt and gain back your control? Think of numerous methods that involve your healing without further hurt inflicted upon anyone else.

The book *Success Is Ele-MENTAL* calls this "successfully revenged." The energy and passion from the painful event are focused on your ability to become massively successful and highly prosperous while removing the source of hurt from your mind. In the book *Elevate Your Mind to Success,* you are taught how to reprogram your mind to automatically focus on success and positive and empowering energy. As long as you let hurtful sources control your mind and continue to focus on them, they will continue to win, no matter what you do. Let them go *completely* and focus on leading a successful, bitter-free, and joyful life unaffected by the negativity of others or thoughts from the past.

How would focusing on healing and building positive and fruitful energy in your own life change your perspective? How would your health and outlook benefit from healing your heart and mind? Has your method of resolving a hurtful event ever involved meditation or prayer? Who is a close friend who will listen without prejudice? How can you be this kind of friend to others? How can you not let pain define and control you? Consider ways you can hold on to your freedom to think as an individual rather than conforming to the guise of others.

7. *Sensitized.* Many things and people are becoming more and more sensitized today. People choose to allow their feelings to be hurt at the slightest sign of discomfort. It appears people lately have been taking things quite personally and becoming "offended" at the slightest verbiage. How are you sensitized by things people say? What can you do not to allow cruel words to affect you personally? Being "offended" is a choice. The one "offended" has now made it their problem, too. How can you evaluate the truth or falsehood of their words?

Perhaps the other person is hurting and does not know how to process their feelings, so they take it out on you. How can you be aware when this occurs? What can you do to instinctively "critically think" about what they have just said and done so you can reveal the truth behind the words or the event? Do you become emotional if things aren't exactly as you would like them to be? Or are you able to be tolerant and forgiving? How can you become more tolerant and forgiving? How could you benefit from becoming this way?

Do you stop and think about both sides of a situation? Or are you quick to react, taking things personally? Or respond like water off of a duck's back, sensing a deeper, underlying issue with the other person, and the problem is actually their problem? How can you become more confident and able to think critically rather than feeling or actually becoming sensitized? Perhaps you could focus on enjoying the world a little more and taking people's actions a little less seriously. How skilled are you at practicing patience and extending grace to others? These can both be very challenging skills to perform! Yet both are extremely admirable qualities to encompass. Both would be incredible qualities to "identify" as, if you must identify at all. Would you like patience, grace, and forgiveness extended to you when you were at fault or in need of compassion?

Realize that "feelings" are a choice you make based on the programming of your thoughts. They do not define you, nor is it wise to base your actions on them. They are unreliable and subject to change circumstantially. Reprogram your mind with solid, objective thoughts that you choose, aligned with your values, and embed them in your mind with your own individually selected program, as defined in *Elevate Your Mind to Success*. Allow this programming to produce automatic, logical responses that parallel your belief system and provide contentedness in your daily life. You will never regret a decision made based on logic. However, a decision based on "feelings" is subject to change based on the situation and can lead to long-lasting regret.

8. *To counter shame or guilt.* Have you ever done something you feel shameful for or maybe ridden with guilt? There are so many of life's lessons to be learned. Some people generally end up learning the hard way! Think of a time or event when you felt ashamed of something you did or said. How about feeling guilty? How did you respond or react during any of these circumstances? Would you react the same way today if another similar situation occurred? How might you respond differently? Have you ever let guilt or shame influence you into doing something boldly to overcome the negative feelings that were attached? How can you critically think about the basis of guilt or shame in an unbiased manner?

STUDENTS: WHO CONNECTS YOUR DOTS?

Is there a link between past treatment you endured and a new desire to define yourself? How can this be an effective way to resolve those feelings? What other alternatives can you think of to create a new vision of an unfortunate occurrence? How can you heal feelings of guilt or shame so that you can react based on logic and reason rather than emotion? How would this be beneficial? Consider the opposing sides of healing versus reacting. Does an attempt to change other people's perspectives change how you view yourself? How are you affected by how others see you? Think about ways to productively heal unfavorable feelings from the past and move forward peacefully and logically, without pressure to react.

9. *Pride.* Pride is said to be one of the most destructive and dangerous qualities. There is a good pride and a bad pride. It is good to be proud of your children or perhaps even your accomplishments or abilities. A positive and upbeat implication is attached to this type of pride, affecting others favorably. The other type of pride carries with it negativity and destructive properties. It is evil-based and self-serving. This type of pride is restrictive, condescending, and poisonous and carries with it the potential, or even desire, to hurt someone else or prove something.

Ask yourself CT questions to understand which sense of pride is in effect. What or who is the source of your pride? What type of energy is attached to the pride, negative or positive vibrations? What is the desired outcome in response to the pride? Does it stem from a place of hurt and pain or a place of joy, contentment, and encouragement? What is the reason for the pride? What is your source of information in the circumstance? Is the intent either to help someone or hurt someone?

Set aside your own personal bias and evaluate the claim. Look at it from different viewpoints. What conclusions do you draw based on the information you collected? What do you think is going on? What information is most important in your determination? How do you know you have all the information? What is your direction in the position you have chosen? How might the stance you are taking affect other people? How do you intend for them to be affected? Analyze your motives, if they are present, and determine your reason for engaging them. Could pride be clouding your judgment in any way? How do you determine the answer to that? How can you address these "feelings" and reprogram your thoughts to positive and uplifting ones if unhealthy pride is involved? Beware of any prideful tendencies, and use logic to reason through the circumstances involved.

Take some time to think critically about the source of the desire to have a defined identity. Or perhaps consider why someone else might be led to this desire. What seems to be the underlying reason for this happening? What or who has led to this decision? What is the expected, or at least desired, outcome? What are the benefits that are linked to having a label? What are the benefits without it? How can you independently establish this decision without influence from anyone else? How would you describe the emotion attached to the decision to define yourself? How can you re-evaluate the situation, remove your bias, and see things from other vantage points? Is your decision full of positive or negative energy? How can you make it all positively energy-based? What is it that you truly want to be known for? Do you want to be defined by a thought? An action? Or what about an ability? Or perhaps an act of service to others or a character quality? How would you like your obituary to be read when it is available to be seen for generations to come? What words of description would you like to be on your tombstone, engraved permanently? Is there still a desire to "identify" as anything? Have you thought of other qualities you possess that would define you better, leaving you feeling uplifted or enlightened?

Critically think about the idea of "identifying" yourself. Think of the pros, cons, and reasons involved. Also, think about why you would choose a certain tag. Consider your answers, opposing answers, and other alternatives from an unbiased perspective. Where does this lead your thoughts?

> *There will always be someone willing to hurt you, put you down, gossip about you, belittle your accomplishments, and judge your soul. It is a fact that we all must face. However, if you realize that God is a best friend Who stands beside you when others cast stones, you will never be afraid, never feel worthless, and never feel alone.*
> —Shannon Alder

> *There are moments when troubles enter our lives, and we can do nothing to avoid them. But they are there for a reason. Only when we have overcome them will we understand why they were there.*
> —Paulo Coelho

> *Every second you dwell on the past, you steal from your future. Every minute you spend focusing on your problems, you take away from finding your solutions.*
> —Robin Sharma

> *I've learned that people will forget what you said, people will forget what you did, but people will never forget how you made them feel.*
> —Maya Angelou

> *Let your hopes, not your hurts, shape your future.*
> —Robert H. Schuller

 Reflect:

1. Are you a person who finds it necessary to define yourself with a label? If so, how do you define yourself?
2. What is the basis, or driving factor, that leads you to this position? Is there positive or negative energy involved? Describe your choices.
3. Do you know others who find it necessary to define themselves with a label? Why do you think some people must define themselves with an "identity"?
4. How do you allow feelings to affect your decisions? In what ways can feelings be unreliable?
5. How has "herd mentality" affected society's need for an "identity"?
6. How do you allow "logic" and "reasoning" to affect your decisions?
7. How have events in your past influenced who you are at this very moment?
8. Think about how you would like to be thought of in years to come. Is your current stance in line with your desired legacy? Are there any changes you would like to make?
9. Write out what you would like your obituary to say. What is your desired legacy? What steps must you take to lay the foundation for this legacy?

CHAPTER 11

Kindness

Kindness is a quality that should be developed and shared with everyone. It should be a part of your everyday life. Kindness is a gentle patience in your interactions with others. Being kind to someone shows you care and respect the other person, especially when it may be difficult to do so. Not everyone you encounter may lead to a pleasant interaction, but it is important to still be the one to show compassion and concern. Show kindness for what is most important to another person. It may involve some sort of sacrifice, such as your time, your expertise, or lending a helping hand.

Compassion is an innate ability to put matters of yourself aside and exhibit heartfelt concern for the feelings of another. Compassion is a form of kindness. There are many ways in which compassion may be displayed.

Ways to show compassion:

1. *With your ears.* The key to understanding the concerns of others is to listen and hear what they are saying. Do not be tempted to make assumptions based on circumstances and presume you know the situation. Allow them to express in their own words what the concerns are fully and the extent of them. Remain silent and let them freely speak, allowing them to vent and hear their concerns out loud as well. Sometimes, hearing the situation out loud already begins the healing process or at least brings about ideas of

resolution. And sometimes, it even makes the situation feel less intense than it initially did in their minds. Be sure to focus on what they are saying rather than formulating how you want to respond. Pay close attention to their words and how they express them.

How can you be a good listener to others? Are you currently a good listener? What are the qualities of a good listener? Describe them. What do you do correctly? What changes can you make to be a better listener? Do you offer a listening ear freely? What is the difference between listening and "hearing"?

2. *With your time.* Time is such a valuable asset, making it a treasured gift to the other person. Giving your time is a generous way to show compassion. It conveys to the other person that you care for them and are willing to focus on their needs. Practicing time-management habits allows you to give your time more freely without compromising your own needs.

How freely do you give your time to others? How valuable is your time? How well do you manage your time? What are you doing well? Where can you improve?

3. *With your heart.* Allow the person to see and feel your concern. Your compassion and kindness will be evident in your face, body expressions, tone of voice, and words. Be authentic. It is comforting to know you are not alone, and these actions bind to the heart of another, providing feelings of strength and unity. Be in the moment with them.

How would you define giving your heart to others? Do you give it willingly and seek to uncover their need? What are ways you can give your heart to someone who is hurting? What if the person is resistant despite their need? How would you respond?

4. *With your words.* After fully listening and gaining insight, offer consoling, confirming, or encouraging words to give them support or enlightenment. They may be in a state of

need of some sort and have just poured out their concerns. Now that their minds are less cluttered by the heavy load they just shared, they may be open to hearing ideas and thoughts about what they revealed. Until they unload their burden, this step may not occur. They may just appreciate some confirmation of what they exposed. Yet once they are drained of the information, their minds are better positioned to expand to more of a solution-seeking mode. Be open and willing to share kind words of compassion.

There is so much power in words. How can you show compassion with your words? How have you shown kindness with your words? Have your words ever "stung"? Have your words ever been misinterpreted when you had good intentions? Describe any of these situations. How can you use words to encourage and uplift others? How can you take advantage of every opportunity to do this?

5. *Your patience.* People may not think rationally when stressed, burdened, grieving, or simply just preoccupied. They may act peculiarly, say unwarranted things, or be overly dramatic. Be patient with them as they work to resolve their issues. Everyone responds to situations differently. Use these steps as a guide to unassumingly help them through their difficult situation at a pace that works best for them. Everyone is going through something—some days are better than others. So, be understanding, especially knowing someday you may need the same kindness shown back to you.

How can you show patience to others? What does this look like to you? Describe the last time you extended patience to someone. Was it hard to do? Did *they* make it hard to do? What did you do well? What would you do differently next time? What improvements can you make?

6. *Your experience.* As a student leader, you have already gained experiences to draw on. They have all led to your ability to lead and be a kind and compassionate person. Continue

to educate yourself and grow your skills and abilities, regardless of age. Draw on this wisdom and provide the most helpful resources or advice possible if warranted and requested. Always remember, sometimes silence is the best answer.

How can you use your experiences to positively help others? What experiences of yours are the most helpful to share with others? How did you acquire them? How can you share them with others most effectively?

7. *Your touch.* Sometimes, the simple act of human touch can flood another with feelings of compassion and concern. Perhaps placing a hand on their shoulder, giving a high-five or fist bump, or a full-on hug of compassion may be appropriate. As people respond differently to touch, ensure you and they are both comfortable with this. It is human nature to want to feel loved and accepted.

You will continually be challenged in life in one way or another. Occurrences often seem to come full circle on a consequential basis. One act of kindness, such as giving your time or a listening ear, will inevitably find its way back to you when you need it the most. Again, this is not the intention, yet it is a wonderful after-effect of a selfless act.

Kindness is a language the deaf can hear, and the blind can see.
—Mark Twain

No act of kindness, no matter how small, is ever wasted.
—Aesop

Compassion is the ultimate expression of love. It is a willingness to show kindness and understanding, even in the face of adversity.
—Jill Fandrich

STUDENTS: WHO CONNECTS YOUR DOTS?

 Reflect:

1. How do you define kindness? What does it look like to you?
2. Name the seven ways listed to show compassion. What can you add to this list?
3. Give five examples of acts of kindness you have seen today. What acts of kindness have you extended today?
4. Give five examples of how you can show kindness to a fellow student.
5. Give five examples of how you can show kindness to family members.
6. Give five examples of how you can show kindness to strangers.
7. Describe your "listening skills." How would you rate them? What is good about them? What could be improved? How can you incorporate better listening skills into all of your interactions? Compare "listening" to "hearing."
8. What changes will you make in your interactions and daily routine to extend more kindness to others?

PART 2

PART 2

CHAPTER 12

Maintaining Your Health

Healthy, Wealthy, and Wise

An attitude of success as a student includes focusing on your health. To be a diligent and productive student and also a leader in any realm, you must be in good health. While information is abundant as to how to stay healthy, this particular chapter will focus on the *importance* of taking the time to maintain good health—change your mindset, and begin to focus on becoming healthy, maintaining good health, or taking appropriate steps to improve your current state of health, as your circumstances allow.

Not everyone is blessed with a clean bill of health. As a matter of fact, people all have their own burdens to carry and endure—unfortunately, some more than others. Everyone is in this together. It is important to help each other in any way you can and encourage others to prioritize their health as well.

So, why is it important for a student to place high importance on health? Health affects your mental capacities and ability to make good and wise decisions. When your body is worn down or not properly cared for, your mind, thoughts, problem-solving abilities, and logical reasoning cannot function in an open, creative, and productive manner. If you strive to be a person in charge in some sort of leadership role, or maybe you already are at some level, people depend on you to perform at your best nearly all the time and take care of yourself physically, mentally, and spiritually. You must be prepared to make wise and sound decisions with the likelihood of favorable outcomes.

Reasons to place high importance on good health:

1. *Your cognitive functions.* Your mind and mental capacities require good health to function at their best. Your ability to reason and problem-solve can be negatively affected by illness, inadequate nutrition, or lack of sleep. Your focusing ability is also affected by your health, and concentrating with clarity occurs more readily when in good health. How does lack of sleep affect your cognitive function? How well do you concentrate with heavy eyelids? How about with a poor diet? When do you have the most clarity? How can you be the most alert? How often do you prioritize caring for your mental capacities? What can you do to improve them?

2. *You influence other people.* People depend on you even as a student, whether in a student organization, a friendship, or in your own household. You are responsible to a certain degree for being a role model for others and making sound decisions and choices that directly affect these people. Many lives depend on you to be at your best and function at a high level. How can you be a positively healthy influence on others? What is your current influence on others regarding being healthy? What are you doing well? Where can improvements be made?

3. *Your business or place of work counts on your productivity.* If you are a working student, your productivity level is tied to your health and mental acuity. Carrying out all of the duties in a place of employment is a large responsibility. It takes lots of hard work and energy to be prolific and excel, and your body and soul are most diligent when caring for your health is a priority. You are responsible for maintaining a healthy mind, body, and soul. Are you showing up to work well-rested and prepared? How do you prepare for work? How do you focus so you can creatively problem-

solve where necessary? Are you prepared to contribute to the team?

4. *Your body systems are complex and need attention.* Your body is amazing, and the fact that it functions as well as it does most of the time is astounding. But it will not last forever. It is imperative to treat it properly, just as you would treat a treasured car or piece of machinery. The more care, maintenance, attention, and time you put into ensuring all systems run properly, the more longevity and ingenuity it will respond with. What is your daily routine of self-care? Describe what you do on a daily basis to care for yourself. What are some obstacles that get in the way? What other ways can you care for yourself? Do you have a regular exercise routine? What do you do if you pull a muscle? What do you do when you feel pain, whether physically or emotionally? Do you allow yourself time for fresh air outdoors and some sunlight? Do you spend too much time in the sun? How do you determine how much is appropriate?

5. *Your quality of life is valuable.* You are responsible for embracing your own quality of life. As mentioned, you will have trials, setbacks, and sometimes unfortunate health-related or disease-related obstacles. And it is miserable to experience days when you do not feel well. It is hard to function in general, let alone function in a resourceful manner, when your health is suffering. You work hard to enjoy the fruits of your labor, yet poor health will decrease the likelihood of a favorable quality-based outcome. Making wise and proactive volitions regarding your health will ensure the best quality of life for your particular circumstances. It is better to figure this all out in your earlier years as opposed to later years when the damage is already done! How do you decide what types of things you put into your body? How do you decide if someone pressures you to consume something that isn't healthy? What things do you

consider before you make a decision? Are you able to make decisions objectively?

6. *The health of relationships is valuable.* Not feeling well can alter your personality and often bring about responses within relationships that may not be favorable, whether negative or simply neglectful. Your patience, emotions, and ability to cope with information or circumstances can be compromised, allowing for possible unpredictable or hard-to-control responses. How do you respond to other people when you are not healthy? How does this differ from when you feel well? How can you ensure healthy responses at all times? What ideas come to mind?

Being or staying healthy is not always easy, especially if you are just getting started. But it is something that must be addressed and routinely tended to. If you have one or many disease states, it is important to find the best care you can and follow up with recommended methods of nutrients and action to control or even eliminate causes or symptoms. Always seek medical advice where you are lacking in the proper information. There are so many sources to choose from. Do your research, seek credible sources, and make the best decisions possible.

How can you place more importance on being healthy? What changes do you need to make? What are you already doing well? Make a list of steps you will take to get started or make improvements.

Nutrition:

Eating properly is a wise decision to keep your body as healthy as possible. Follow appropriate guidelines and eat a healthy diet. Your body needs various foods and nutrients to perform at its best. The right nutrients, minerals, vitamins, etc., will help strengthen and fortify your body. There are many approaches to finding the best eating plan for your age and body type and considering issues your body may have. Consider them all, make wise choices, and seek a healthcare professional where appropriate. As your body's immune system is its

STUDENTS: WHO CONNECTS YOUR DOTS?

best defense against diseases and illnesses, focus on building *natural* immunity. An example of a healthy preventative daily regimen of supplements to build your immune system considering current world events includes quercetin 500 mg, zinc 50-100 mg, vitamin C 3000 mg, vitamin D3 2,500 IU, magnesium 500 mg, then melatonin 3-10mg at bedtime. Other supplements that may be considered are selenium 200 mg, niacin 100 mg (watch for flushing), CoQ10 300 mg, calcium 500 mg, and vitamin B12 1000 mcg daily, to name a few. Be sure to *verify age-related dosages* with a healthcare professional.

Avoid unfavorable vices, such as smoking, alcohol, illicit drugs, vaccinations, or any other drug that is not needed to help a disease state in your body. Your body sees them as foreign objects and may harm different body processes that may not be evident immediately, including your mind. Drink lots of water, avoid excessive sugary snacks, and be selective with what you put into your body.

Describe your current diet. How did you select it? Do you feel it is well-rounded? How do you feel? Are there any changes you need to make? Is your diet lacking in any category? How can you ensure you are getting all the necessary *natural* nutrients your body needs?

Exercise:

Get moving! Exercise is also very important to keep your body limber and blood flowing properly to and from the heart. It does become difficult to exercise when your body changes and becomes more complicated. Sometimes, certain disease states or ailments prevent us from exercising in ways we find easy or the most enjoyable. Adjust and find out what your body is capable of doing. Different machines can be placed under a desk or chair that could lightly get your feet moving, such as a mini stair-stepper or elliptical. Attach Velcro weights to your ankles or lift light weights, use stretch bands for resistance, or even use your body's own resistance to move and stretch. Build up your body with push-ups, sit-ups, and pull-ups. If you are healthy, there is no excuse not to instigate a healthy exercise regimen. Do research and ask trained professionals in physical therapy, a coach, or a workout trainer how to best work with your circumstances. But whatever it takes, get moving and get your blood circulating with proper oxygenation to all systems in your body, especially your brain and heart. You need to stay as limber as possible to be at your peak performance.

What is your favorite way to exercise? How did this become your favorite? Do you have more than one favorite? Name them all. How often do you exercise? How does exercise affect your health overall? How do you feel when you don't exercise for a while? What is your motivating factor to exercise? Do you exercise willingly or out of guilt? Are you part of a team? How else can you add more exercise to your life? Do you take the stairs when possible? Explain the importance of stretching out and preparing properly for different sports or activities.

Do not give in to excuses. Successful students drop the blame game and refuse to hide behind excuses. Take control of your life and circumstances and take responsibility for your actions and the outcomes. If something happened to you outside your control, accept exactly where you are right now, be accountable for however you got there, and take responsibility for how you *respond*. Be amenable to maintaining if you are exactly where you want to be or devise a plan to move forward, make adjustments or improvements if not, and get on track to get to where you want to be. There are no excuses when it comes to professional growth and leadership. There are issues and circumstances, but take them at face value and find solutions. It is brave and honorable to admit when you are wrong and then take action to make it right. As there is no room for excuses at this level, you must be in a cognizant frame of mind, healthy and alert, ready to find solutions, problem-solve, and create your own pathway to success.

The road to success is bumpy and difficult, filled with potholes and detours. You need every advantage you can possibly have on this strategic and exciting adventure. It is wise to focus on your health first so you can be clearly mindful of the responsibilities surrounding you. This, along with determination, drive, and lots of action, will lead to a healthy, wealthy, and productive outcome. Some may even say *health IS wealth*. So be wise, be healthy, and therefore, be wealthy. Healthy body, healthy mind, wealthy soul.

> *He who has health has hope, and he
> who has hope has everything.*
> —Thomas Carlyle

> *Health is a state of complete harmony
> of the body, mind, and spirit.*
> —B. K. S. Iyengar

> *It is health that is real wealth and
> not pieces of gold and silver.*
> —Mahatma Gandhi

> *Nurturing yourself is not selfish – it's essential
> to your survival and your well-being.*
> —Renee Peterson Trudeau

 Reflect:

1. How do you define healthy? What does it look like to you?
2. Describe how important your health is to you. What steps do you take to stay healthy? Are you currently doing anything that negatively affects your body? If so, describe. What can you do differently?
3. Describe your current diet. Is it a well-balanced diet? What can you change to improve it? What are you already doing correctly?
4. Name five ways staying healthy can positively affect you.
5. What is your favorite form of exercise? How often do you exercise? How can you incorporate more activity into your daily or weekly routine?

6. What changes to your current lifestyle can you make to improve your health or future outcome? How can you positively impact the health of others?

7. Name five challenges that affect your health in some way. How can you overcome these obstacles?

CHAPTER 13

Who's to Blame?

Have you noticed more finger-pointing in the world around you today than ever before? Very few, or perhaps almost no one, seem to be at fault for all the issues around you, professionally as well as personally, yet everyone is blaming everyone else as the one at fault. Taking responsibility for one's own actions is becoming a rare occurrence, yet it is a highly regarded and impressive attribute to encompass. Blame is a claim that someone other than yourself is responsible for a certain act, cause, situation, or, lately, even a *feeling* one experiences. There are even movements occurring based on the belief that "it" was someone else's fault. It is time to think critically about the concept of partaking in the same action of blaming others and looking at the actual source leading to this potential action.

Reasons why people choose to blame others:

1. *Fear.* Fear covers a large array of territory, including some of the points that follow. *False-Events-Appearing-Real* is a crippling feeling that causes people to do or say unfortunate or unnecessary things. What is the fear? Is there fear of reprisal for not turning in an assignment? Fear of feeling inadequate? Where does the fear stem from? What is the worst-case scenario if the fear comes to fruition? Recalling that a fear is something that has not actually happened, what are possible situations that may occur? How likely are

they to occur? What evaluation can be performed to shed light on alternatives? Who is involved with this fear? What result is desired from choosing to blame others in a situation based on a fear? What ways could be chosen to be more productive? What if the choice could be made to focus on a solution rather than a fear? What could this possibly hurt? Or could it be helpful? How could the fear be overcome? What methods are currently being used? How can all bias be taken out of a scenario in order to find a productive solution rather than blame someone? What if the situation was in reverse? How would you handle unwarranted blame due to a fear being placed on you? How can you create a situation with positive energy where it becomes instinctive to seek solutions rather than choose a defensive stance? How could this improve the environment around you? How would this change your classroom or workplace atmosphere? How can you identify fears, reason them out, and eliminate them?

2. *Guilt.* Guilt may leave an empty and anxious feeling looming inside. Guilt could lead to blaming someone else for something that occurred, with the possible result of temporarily relieving the anxiety. What is the basis of the guilt? Where does it stem from? What are the circumstances that surround the situation? How can the guilt be resolved in an unbiased way, within your own means? What have you learned from the situation? How would you respond differently next time? What would the premise be of blaming someone else for an issue due to feelings of guilt? What are other ways that the situation could be dealt with without blaming someone else? What is the truth in the situation? How do you handle feelings of guilt? Is there a need to step back and resolve any situations of guilt? How has this shaped your decisions? How can logic and reasoning be utilized in reframing the guilt? What conclusions can you draw for an effective resolution?

3. *Pride.* Could the "hurtful" type of pride (not the innocent pride of accomplishment) be a reason for choosing to blame someone else? What are the surrounding circumstances of the pride? How did the situation of blame arise? What are some alternate ways to respond rather than blaming someone else? Who is involved in the circumstance involving pride? What is a response that could lead to a productive outcome? Evaluate the situation. What are all of the circumstances that have led to the response? How did the response fit the evaluated information? What is the desired outcome of the reaction? How can pride be addressed in order to resolve the negative feelings attached to it? Often, a temporary "good" feeling will still leave you empty or hurting once again, as the issue itself has not been resolved, such as if the feelings were reframed and properly healed. How can you decipher the source of the pride? How can you heal negative feelings so there is a lasting resolution? What if you tried to resolve the source in order to heal rather than react and rebuke?

4. *Hurt.* Hurt can lead to many responses, one of which can be lashing out and blaming someone else. Has someone who was hurting ever "lashed out" and blamed you for something? How did you handle this situation? Was this ever a pathway you chose? Who was involved in this interaction? How did this resolve the issue? Have you ever allowed hurt to be a reason for you to blame someone else for something? How do you rationalize this decision? What type of research was performed before you made this decision? What is the basis of the decision? What other options for resolution are there? How could you respond differently? What would happen if you resolved the hurt feelings first? What alternative approaches could you take to handle the situation? Have you ever had a successful outcome by blaming someone else? Have you viewed the situation from an opposing perspective? How did you

choose the person you picked to blame? How did they hurt you? How will you logically move past the hurt?

5. *Insecurity.* Have you ever blamed someone due to an insecurity you had or have? Who was involved in the circumstance? What role did they play? What were the circumstances that led to this decision? What research did you perform to reach the decision on which to act? What are some alternative choices that could've been made? What is the insecurity? How has this affected your life? What steps have you taken in an attempt to eliminate the insecurity? How did you evaluate the steps it would take? Who could help with the source of the insecurity? How did you justify your responses? Would you choose a different way to respond? How has an insecurity caused you to respond in other circumstances? Have you been able to find a way to take control of the insecurity? How will you logically resolve the insecurity?

6. *Peer pressure.* Peer pressure is a consistent and repetitious force that will always be a contention in our lives. Have you ever allowed pressure from someone else to cause you to blame another person for something? How did you reach a decision to do this? Who was involved in the circumstance? Were they actually guilty or not? How did you respond when the decision was made? What would have been an alternate way to respond? How often do you hand over control to someone else due to pressure? How can you be more aware when you are being pressured and step back to think about the situation critically from an unbiased perspective? Have you ever been the recipient of blame due to a peer pressure situation? How was it resolved? How can you overcome someone else's influence and make your own decisions?

7. *Irresponsibility.* Everyone has been brought up differently and under differing circumstances. What were your circumstances like? What type of emphasis was placed on being responsible? Who was involved in developing

your character? How much emphasis was placed on this development? Have you ever blamed someone in order to "dodge" responsibility? What are ways in which this could happen? How could it be prevented? What are ways you can develop the character quality of being responsible? How can you take responsibility for your actions? How are others affected if you aren't responsible for your actions? What benefits are involved with being responsible? What consequences might occur if you did not take responsibility for your actions? How do the people that surround you respond when the responsibility is theirs? What would happen if you made this a steadfast quality in your life? What could the benefits be?

8. *Unaccountability.* Have you ever been in a situation where someone was not accountable for their actions, and it negatively affected you? Who was involved? How did you respond? What were the consequences? Has there been a time when you were not accountable for your actions? Have you ever blamed someone when the accountability was actually your responsibility? What were the circumstances surrounding this event? Who was involved? How was the recipient affected by your decision? What are other ways you could have responded? What are some possible different outcomes? How can you evaluate each of these scenarios? How could the situation have been handled better? How can you be more accountable for your actions and your words? It's important to be accountable for yourself. It takes integrity and an authentic person to accept accountability for all of the actions that are chosen by you. How can you program this quality into your mind to become an automatic response?

9. *Reputation.* Sometimes, to spare a reputation, people may choose to blame someone else for something they have done. Has this ever happened to you? Has someone ever blamed you for something they did in order to protect their reputation? How did you handle the situation? Have

you ever blamed someone else for something to protect your reputation? In either case, what was the outcome? Who was involved in the blame? What are some better alternatives regarding how the situation could have been addressed? How do you wish you had responded? In what ways could the result be positive for both sides? How did you find yourself in the predicament to begin with? How was the other person affected? In what ways can you avoid a future occurrence like this? What have you learned about the situation?

10. *Uneducated or uninformed.* Lack of education can be an element leading to blame. Have you ever been inflicted with blame by someone who didn't fully understand a situation? How about the reverse circumstance? Have you ever blamed someone else before you had all of the facts? How did you expect the outcome to play out? How did it actually turn out? Who was involved in this circumstance? What choices could you have made differently? How many options did you entertain before you made your decision on how you responded? How much and what kind of research did you do in preparation for your action? How could you become better informed about the situation? What would you change about your responses? How can you use this information for future situations? Has education, or lack thereof, been a problem before in making decisions? How do you keep yourself current on information? Do you gather all facts from your side, as well as the opposing side, before you come to a conclusion? How can you program this type of thinking into your mind for automatic responses?

11. *Personality types.* People with different personality types can choose certain and almost predictable responses. Narcissists, for example, are notorious for blaming anyone in their pathway for anything they can think of. They are rarely, if ever, accountable for anything. It seems they are never wrong about anything in their eyes. Other toxic personality types respond the same way. Be aware of who

you are involved with and the potential for blame against you that may occur. How could a blame scenario with toxic personality types be avoided? What steps could you take to protect yourself? How much do you know about toxic personality types? Do you have one of these personalities? How would you respond in either case? How can you focus on the facts at hand and allow them to be the focus of the responses using an unbiased perspective? What education might be helpful to learn more about this topic? How do you recognize this personality type?

12. *Shame.* Have you ever been on the receiving end of blame, involving shame felt by another person? How did you handle this situation? What were the surrounding circumstances? Has shame ever driven you to blame someone else for something? What would be the premise of this action? What would be the expected outcome of blaming someone else? How could it be avoided? What is the source of shame? How can that be resolved? How can the feeling of shame be identified, understood, and dealt with to resolution? In what ways can this be avoided in the future? What do you know about shame? How can you help someone else who feels a sense of shame? What information can be researched to deal with this feeling in a healthy way?

13. *Financial incentive.* Has a financial incentive, either profitable or costly, ever been a reason used to blame someone else? Has someone blamed you for something, with finances being the influencing factor of the blame? Money can be very influential. What are ways you could see money affecting people? How might the influence of money cause someone to place blame on someone else? What might be the expected outcome? How can you ensure money is never used as an excuse to blame someone else? What would be the benefits of securing a plan? Do you know anyone who placed blame on someone else due to a monetary matter? How did the matter transpire? How could this have been better handled? What are the possible

outcomes for this person? What did you learn from this experience? *Follow the money.*

14. *Justification.* People are capable of many sorts of things in their pursuit to justify themselves or their actions. Has anyone ever blamed you for something for the sake of their justification? Have you ever blamed someone else in order to justify something? Who was involved? What was the premise of the need to justify? What was the expected outcome of blaming someone else? Was the desired result received? What other choices could have been made? How would a change in previous decisions change the outcome? What could be done differently? Was the issue that needed to be resolved ever properly accounted for? What can be learned from this situation?

Blame is more and more common in all facets of life. It even occurs based on historical events that are not even in existence today. What might be the reasons someone would place blame for something that happened in the past? How would a past event not brought on by any people currently today be a reason to place fault on someone today? What reasoning is used to justify blame for events of the past in the current setting? How might this situation look to those who are being blamed that were not in past events? How are they, or are they not, really at fault?

How would it look if the situation was evaluated from the opposing side? What evidence is there to link today's people with the actions of the past? What is the expected outcome of the action of blaming? What is the premise of the action? What has led to this action? What can be learned from history? How does blaming a historical event on current events today change anything? Does erasing the past make the events not real anymore? Or did they still really happen? What are alternative ways to handle the situation? What is a more productive response that can lead to a supportive and favorable current or future perspective? How can this be positively applied to your lifestyle today? Are you able to learn and grow because of it? How can you resolve any potential negative feelings and transform the energy into positive and productive energy?

Blame is an ineffective way to resolve any situation. It is a defensive stance that is counterintuitive to a resolution. How can you find alternative ways to view a situation? What other methods can you think of to resolve hurt feelings due to a past or other painful situation? What are the reasons for taking it personally, even if you were not personally there? What might happen if you had the courage to accept your life choices and where you are right now? If you are unhappy with the scenario, what productive and positive changes can you make in your life to improve your situation?

How can you find enjoyment in life without focusing on anyone else and needing to blame someone? What are your gifts and talents? How can you use them in a fun, useful, and creative way? What activities do you enjoy? What is something you have always desired to accomplish or succeed in? What would it take to pursue this dream?

How can you learn more about accountability? Take responsibility for your actions. Be confident in who you are and where you are. Learn to think for yourself, without prejudice, focus on self-improvement, and make choices that lead to true and continuous joy rather than temporary "happiness." Blame may provide a brief satisfaction as it "justifies" a hurt, but this temporary happiness is subject to circumstances. At the same time, no one can take your joy away. Joy is a sustainable state of contentedness based on faith, hope, and security regarding what is to come, not based on a temporary past or current, circumstantial event. Seek to fill your life with joy.

> *All blame is a waste of time. No matter how much fault you find with another, and regardless of how much you blame him, it will not change you. The only thing blame does is keep the focus off you when you are looking for external reasons to explain your unhappiness or frustration. You may succeed in making another feel guilty about something by*

blaming him, but you won't succeed in changing whatever it is about you that is making you unhappy.
—Wayne Dyer

You can either blame everybody else, or you can take a look at yourself and determine where you can improve.
—Robert Kiyosaki

If you could kick the person in the pants responsible for most of your trouble, you wouldn't sit for a month.
—Theodore Roosevelt

You will never become who you want to be if you keep blaming everyone else for who you are now.
—John Spence

You can get discouraged many times, but you are not a failure until you begin to blame somebody else and stop trying.
—John Burroughs

 Reflect:

1. Are you a person who finds it necessary to blame yourself or others? If so, what might be a better way to approach a situation?
2. What driving factor may lead you to consider blaming someone else for something you did or experienced?
3. Think of someone you know who tends to blame others. Now think of someone who takes on all their own responsibility and is always accountable for their actions. Compare and contrast the differences between the two. What do you notice?

4. Looking at two or more sides to a story, what might be an appropriate approach to take in a difficult situation?
5. How have events in your past influenced how you perceive blame?
6. Think about how you would like to be thought of in years to come. Is your current view regarding blame in line with your desired legacy? Are there any changes you would like to make?
7. How can you be productive and incorporate the positive character qualities of responsibility and accountability into your programming?
8. Critically think about the concept of blame. What comes to mind?

CHAPTER 14

How Do You Communicate?

Speaking:

How do you speak to others? Do you look them in the eye, speak clearly, and wait your turn within the dialogue? Or do you speak quietly, mumbling your words just to get them out quickly? When engaging with others in a conversation, it is important to speak clearly and solidly project your voice, avoiding a wavering and weak or even a quivering tone. Learn to be confident in your speech and be aware that you are loud enough to be heard while not being so overbearing that you evade the conversations of others or, supposedly, quiet environments.

    Enunciate your words and ensure you use proper grammar and punctuation markers, such as an elevation in tone as you ask a question or excitement as you congratulate someone. Not only are your words important, but also how they are presented. Are you speaking in person or on the phone? Is the phone up to your ear, or are you on speakerphone? Are you using AirPods or some other listening or speaking device? Ensure there is clarity in any means chosen.

    Pay close attention to your body language and allow it to match the conversation and environment. Learn when to be relaxed and when to display professionalism and charisma. Are you slouching and uninterested? Or are you attentive and "tuned in"? What is your actual demeanor? How do you carry yourself? How confident are you? How effective are you in your communication? Do you know

STUDENTS: WHO CONNECTS YOUR DOTS?

how much "speaking" your arms and hands are doing? It is natural to have movement in them as you speak, yet ensure it isn't so excessive that it becomes distracting.

One way to determine the situation is to be alert to your surroundings and those around you. Quiet your mind and be observant. As a student and future leader, there are many opportunities to be taken advantage of or areas that may be overlooked and need your due diligence. Or even unexpected and untapped possibilities within your grasp, waiting to be discovered.

Areas in which to be alert:

1. *Your environmental surroundings.* Be mindful of your environment. Are you in a casual or professional situation? Is the volume appropriate? How about acoustics or ergonomics? Is the equipment functioning properly if it will be used? Is there anything surrounding you that may distract your attention? How can you counter this effect?

2. *Your "people" surroundings.* What are the people like around you? Should they be there? Are there any that are missing? How are they behaving, and is it appropriate under the circumstances? How do they speak? Are they healthy, focused, and vibrant, or sickly and distant? Are they confident and motivated? What are they revealing through their body language? Are they alert and useful? Are they hurting? What are their needs, and can you meet them? How can you positively affect or encourage them?

3. *The timeframe.* Do the person or people you are engaging with appear to be in a rush? What are ways you can assess the time necessity involved? Are you in a hurry? Has there been an allotted timeframe for the interaction? Are there any time constraints you are aware of? Ensure you assess the situation, as time is a very precious asset!

4. *Your attire.* Are you dressed appropriately for the interaction? How were you informed about the "dress code"? Did you

research ahead of time? Be aware of every detail and make sure it's appropriate. Is your shirt buttoned, pants zipped, and shoes tied? Are you casual or formal? Pay attention to details.

5. *Your appearance.* Is your hair combed or washed, for that matter? Are you showered and properly groomed? Are you thinking properly or disheveled? Do you feel you look proper for the situation? Are your teeth brushed? How did you fashionably prepare for the interaction? Are you calm or enthusiastic about the venue as appropriate?

6. *The goals of the interaction.* What are your objectives in the interaction? Are they clearly defined? What are the goals of the other person? What do you anticipate? Are you on the same page? Are you prepared?

7. *Means of communication.* How will you be communicating? Will it be face-to-face? Or verbally by phone? Perhaps it is by Zoom or some other type of webcast or podcast. Are you prepared? Is any necessary equipment intact? Do you have all the electronics modified as necessary? Is the lighting bright or warm enough? What is the background like? Will it distract from you or the message? What else can you do to prepare? Ensure you can be clearly heard and seen if appropriate.

8. *You.* What is your demeanor like? How will you respond to favorable situations? How about difficult or challenging ones? Are you slow to anger and quick to forgive? Are you open to suggestions? Empathetic to the needs of others? Intimidating or likable? How is your health? Do you know the importance of proper nutrition, exercise, and sleep? Do you allow enough downtime and a healthy balance of professional, personal, and spiritual time? Do you have more to give? Or perhaps, do you give too much? Are you doing what needs to be done? Are you aware of what needs to be done? Are you alert and well-prepared? What other ways can you prepare yourself for the interaction?

STUDENTS: WHO CONNECTS YOUR DOTS?

Authentic leaders have an innate ability to sense when something "just isn't right." When you are more tuned in, healthy, and alert, you possess a keen awareness and are able to identify discrepancies in how things should be. You will be more precise in your decision-making abilities and communication, and you will be able to determine if situations are fair and compromises are amenable. Or if people are sincere or perhaps less than truthful. And you are less likely to be scammed or taken advantage of. You are most useful and effective when you are alert and prepared.

Review the past week in your mind. Are there any areas educationally where you now see you weren't as alert as you could've been? How about personally or spiritually? What changes can you make today to integrate this character quality into your ongoing list of favorable attributes?

How would you describe your speaking abilities this past week? Which opportunities stand out favorably? Why do you feel this way? Are there any speaking engagements you feel didn't go so well? Explain why you think this way. What did you do well? What will you improve for next time? How will you make these changes?

Listening:

Would you like to be the most captivating person in the room? How do you become this most endearing and sought-after person? While there are numerous ways to go about this, we will discuss one way in particular, and the answer is simple...by LISTENING! Active listening. Often, people take an incorrect approach in an attempt to be noticed and spend a great deal of time talking about themselves, trying to impress others with their outstanding accomplishments. While their resume may be astounding and accolades are very much deserved, this approach is rarely, if ever, effective. This type of self-talk may lead to envy from the listener or the release of a "topper," which is trying to one-up what the other person has said.

It is just human nature to love to talk about yourself. After all, you are amazing. And you are beautifully and wonderfully made. It is an innate sense you are born with to want to talk about yourself, and as you know, it is a topic in which you are best informed and most knowledgeable. You may enjoy talking about yourself or your circumstances for many reasons.

Reasons you may want to talk about yourself:

1. *You know yourself.* There is no easier topic to discuss than the one you know the best. It is often difficult for people to converse with others if the topic is unknown. Some people are good at making up a conversation as they go along and find common ground. Others may be unable to "create and relate" and find unknown conversations intimidating. This may lead to a conversation focused on yourself.
2. *Your mind is actively in the midst of events.* It is easy to discuss situations you are already in the middle of. Your own life is actively happening, and it is, therefore, easy to discuss events that are currently underway with someone else. They are at the forefront of your mind. "Current events" are popular topics of conversation; nothing is more current than your everyday present life. It may be the morning you just experienced with your family or an episode at school. These are the topics that are currently in your thoughts.
3. *The desire to problem solve.* Everyone needs to vent; sometimes, you may not come into contact with someone familiar very often to share the events cluttering your mind. It is human nature to interact with others, and an intimate form of that is sharing your personal experiences with each other. It is often difficult to undertake some things yourself, so talking them over with another person is therapeutic. Often, just hearing yourself say the issue aloud causes solutions to stir in your mind. It is a beneficial form of problem-solving.
4. *Unawareness.* Some people just do not take the time to see the whole picture. Based on the previous three reasons, you might be inclined to monopolize a conversation focused on

yourself, just not realizing the recipient of your discussion has needs and a message they would like to convey. This is not a selfish motive but rather out of either a lack of awareness of sharing or a deep need to declutter your mind and, as a result, disregard a potential need of the person you are speaking to.

5. *Cognitive issues.* Sometimes, there is a memory deficit, and recalling information regarding the other person is difficult. This can be an embarrassing situation as it could appear the recipient is unimportant, which is not the case at all. It may be easier to engage in self-talk in order to have information to discuss and possibly to avoid the embarrassment of unintentionally forgetting information that should be relevant.

6. *The recipient of your conversation is already trained to be a captivator.* Perhaps your conversation partner is already educated on how to be captivating. He or she may be directing the conversation to be all about you, leading you to proceed with talking exclusively about yourself. This would include unawareness, as mentioned before, or perhaps you are aware and are just responding kindly to the questions presented in the conversation with a person who truly cares about you and is interested in hearing you share more information.

7. *Self-centered or narcissistic.* It happens. Many people have a love of self. Or they love to hear themselves speak. Most likely, it is all about themselves. This is a particular personality trait in which a person has little or no concern for anyone else. Despite your potential interjection in a conversation to make it a two-way sharing of information, they quickly and inevitably redirect the conversation to everything that involves themselves. They truly do not want to hear any information about anyone else. And they certainly do not want your advice on anything they speak of. A quick note about this type of person—when you have identified this type, you can be polite and listen, not expecting to share

in the conversation, but at the first opportunity, gently yet quickly exit the conversation and avoid future contact, as this personality type is very dangerous.

You will always make a much better impression by allowing others to speak about themselves and be heard. Think about it logically. What is your favorite topic when speaking with someone else? Most people, if being honest, would say something about themselves, such as their interests, abilities, family, goals, events in their lives, etc. That all makes sense. So, how should you do this if you want to engage someone else in a conversation they find interesting? Focus on them.

How to be captivating through conversation:

1. If you are initiating the conversation, begin by asking questions about them. If you wish to network and meet new people and make a lasting impression, approach another person with questions about that person that would delight them. You could observe something they are wearing, something you overheard them say, or something you know they did. This will give that person an opportunity in a positive setting to expand on a gratifying conversation regarding their favorite topic: themselves. What are some questions you can think of to ask the other person? How can you get them to talk about themselves? How will you draw out their interests?

2. Make direct yet comfortable eye contact with the recipient. If the conversation is in person, look the other person in the eyes, especially the right eye. Make it a soft focus, and do not let the surroundings distract you from giving them your attention. Let them be the center of the conversation and allow them to feel that what they say is important and you listen attentively.

3. Interject comments or questions to show interest. By interacting in the conversation with comments on content, asking questions for clarification, or even giving occasional

STUDENTS: WHO CONNECTS YOUR DOTS?

nods, the other person engaged with you in conversation will know you are listening and that what they say is important to you. What are some interjections you could make? How could this be effective? What other questions could you ask?

4. If you are asked questions about yourself, politely answer, then continue with questions about them. Turn the conversation back to the other person and get them to talk more about themselves. The person asking the questions is the one in control of the conversation. How might turning the conversation back to the other person pique their interest? How else can you turn the conversation back to them?

5. Be kind, nonjudgmental, intentional, and smile. Be sincere and mean what you say and say what you mean. Always be kind and interested in your conversations. Smile and use appropriate expressions to display your interest. Time and a listening ear are some of the greatest gifts you can give someone. How can you show kindness in a conversation? What other ways can you show interest?

There are many ways to become the most captivating person in the room. Here, we focused on conversations and how to be viewed as having an enticing quality, even if you spoke the least! There is a time and a place in close friendships or business interactions for two-way conversations, but this is directed at building a reputation as a captivating or alluring person of interest. It is not always what we say. Sometimes, what we don't say, or rather, what we hear or listen to, defines us the most.

Good communication is the bridge
between confusion and clarity.
—Jill Fandrich

Speak clearly, if you speak at all; carve
every word before you let it fall.
—Oliver Wendell Holmes

> *Listen with the intent to understand,*
> *not the intent to reply.*
> —Stephen R. Covey

 Reflect:

1. Describe your view of "good" communication skills. How would you describe your own current communication style? How would you describe your speaking skills?
2. What are you doing well? Where can you improve?
3. Who do you know who has excellent communication skills? Describe what makes them excellent. What can you learn from them? How can you practice these skills?
4. What have you learned about being a captivating person? How would you rate your current listening skills? How can you improve your listening skills?
5. How would you describe your nonverbal communication skills? What are you doing well? Where could you improve?
6. How can you show kindness in all of your communication interactions? How can you be more aware of why a recipient might communicate the way they are?
7. What did you learn in this chapter that you never thought of before?
8. What other thoughts do you have about effective communication?

CHAPTER 15

Volunteering and Serving Others

Acknowledging the many blessings in your life and responding with gratitude is important. This can be in the form of "paying forward" by volunteering and serving others. There is always someone in life who is not as fortunate as you. You have a perfect opportunity to find a need and meet it. Make this a habit in your life at an early age. Let it be a part of your everyday life to be aware of the needs of others and seek to meet their needs, one person at a time.

Volunteering and serving others are important because they allow you to contribute to the betterment of your communities and society as a whole. Volunteering can help address important social issues, such as poverty, hunger, homelessness, loneliness, and environmental conservation. Volunteering also allows you to connect with and support marginalized or vulnerable populations, providing much-needed assistance and compassion. You can build empathy and understanding by serving others. You develop a sense of responsibility and citizenship.

Additionally, volunteering and serving others can positively impact mental and emotional well-being. Studies have shown that those who volunteer experience lower rates of depression and overall improved mental health. In essence, as you are giving, you are ultimately and unintentionally receiving as well.

Volunteering can also provide a sense of purpose and fulfillment as you see the tangible impact of your efforts in the lives of those you serve. Overall, volunteering and serving others are important because they promote compassion, empathy, and a sense of community, ultimately leading to a more cohesive and caring society.

Volunteering is an appropriate way to show you are grateful. Be content and grateful for everything you have. Demonstrate heartfelt appreciation to others when they are a part of this. Count your benefits rather than your burdens. Do you take things for granted or take things for gratitude? Unfortunately, some people can misinterpret an opportunity for gratefulness with a feeling of entitlement. Entitlement has no place in a true leader. Consider everything a blessing and respond with gracious appreciation. Consider serving others an honor. Display an *attitude of gratitude* and allow it to brighten your outlook.

Gratefulness can either be felt internally for your own current blessings or reflected and shown to someone else for something of their instigation or initiation. No matter the source, take advantage of the opportunity to express thankfulness for this enlightening treasure. How can you show more gratitude daily? How many opportunities can you think of that passed you by today to show gratitude? Compare and contrast entitlement and gratefulness. What do you notice? How can you show more appreciation throughout your day? What opportunities can you identify to volunteer and serve others?

Effects of gratefulness through volunteering or serving others:

1. *Connectedness.* With feelings of gratitude, you feel connected with those involved. There is a sense of unity and community, and you realize we are all in this together.
2. *Inspiration.* Gratefulness transforms energy into positive vibrations, leading to inspiration and maybe even aspirations. You feel inspired to pay forward or pass it on. The positive energy is infectious and flows through all your body's cells, affecting other people in your immediate

STUDENTS: WHO CONNECTS YOUR DOTS?

environment. Take advantage of the inspiration, use it as motivation, and allow your mind to expand with productive imagination.

3. *Support.* Comfort is an effect of gratefulness. You feel supported and maybe even emboldened by a sustained sense of confidence. There is an essence of security as well.

4. *Invigoration.* Serving others is invigorating and causes you to feel energized. It arouses a desire to be a positive light for more people, just as you are enlightened and enlivened. It stimulates your senses and gives life and spirit to your mind. You are awakened from the mundane and revived with a strong and vitalized feeling, stimulating your desire to further share this blessing with others.

5. *Value.* Your sense of value is revealed through volunteering, both giving and receiving. You feel worthwhile and significant in your purpose. You also feel the value and distinction of others when you show this gratefulness to and for them. You recognize their importance and the value of letting them know the magnitude of their worth.

6. *Fulfillment.* A feeling of being fulfilled or even nourished is an effect of serving. Something amazing has been accomplished or completed, leading to content satisfaction. Or perhaps the event or gesture is minor, but you have the ability to accept it as a treasured gift and value a deeper appreciation. Unsettled feelings are enigmatically sustained and even elevated.

7. *Appreciation.* Serving others provides a feeling of appreciation from both a giving and receiving perspective. When you show gratitude, appreciation inevitably follows. You feel relished and maybe even admired. Share the same sense of appreciation with others.

8. *Blessing.* Feeling blessed and being a blessing are effects of serving others. Your mind and senses are enveloped with pleasure or contentment. You are delighted and feel empowered by choosing to be a grateful servant.

9. *Transformation.* The positive energy engaged by volunteering can transform your attitude and vantage point. Your mind may declutter as it releases negativity and allows supportive and peaceful thoughts to freely and loosely flow, leading to a favorable and energized demeanor.
10. *Astonishment.* Serving others can lead to astonishment. When you appreciate even the smallest detail, your ability to value things or situations can be immensely altered for the better. You may find more value and regard in what used to be ordinary. You gain a more mature acceptance and appreciation for the simplest things and experience pure joy and contentment.
11. *Purpose.* With a serving spirit, you feel a sense of purpose. It's as though everything suddenly makes sense, and you are exactly where you need to be and doing what you were created to do. You found a worthy purpose and an intention for your actions. You feel settled and accomplished and are awakened to your meaningful life.

In what ways do you volunteer? Where do you see occasions to volunteer? Are there opportunities in your neighborhood to help others? How often do you offer your time or services? What does this entail? How long have you been serving others in some capacity? What other ways can you serve others? How do you feel about serving others? How are you inspired or invigorated by serving?

Volunteering and serving others displays generosity. Generosity is the willingness to give of yourself, such as time or resources, to help another while expecting nothing in return. It is a selfless act, and sometimes even sacrificial, for the benefit of others. It could be for a specific person, organization, or event needing volunteers, such as a local church or soup kitchen. Optimize generosity in whatever means you can. There are many different methods and opportunities to be generous.

STUDENTS: WHO CONNECTS YOUR DOTS?

Ways to be generous:

1. *With your time.* Your time is one of your most precious assets. It is a generous gift to share your time with others, especially when they have a need. If you live an organized life, you can find ways to share your time, even if it involves rearranging your schedule or asking support staff for additional help. How can you organize your day so you have time to share with others? Is this something you do already? How often do you share your time with others? Are you aware of others sharing their time with you?

2. *With your money.* Loaning, gifting, or donating money is the most obvious source of generosity. If possible, offer it as a free gift with no expectations in return. You will be rewarded at some point for your kindness. As you are selfless, God will always find a way to respond generously in return, although you should not be waiting in expectation. If it is an agreed-upon loan, be gentle and sincere in the terms, always understanding there may be a chance you will never see this money again. Only provide what you are willing and comfortable never to see again. In a sense, it is also a "gift." Once you release it, let go of any tension or connection to the money. And if it is returned, consider it a blessing.

    It is also Biblical to tithe 10% of the first fruits of your income to God. Be generous, and do not hesitate to offer more if you are financially able. You can never outgive God! How often are you generous with your money? In what ways can you be generous with it? Think critically when it comes to the choices you make, and always ensure you are wise with your money.

3. *With your talents.* You have been blessed with your own unique talents and abilities. Use these gifts to bless and help someone else any time you can. Your gifts are meant to be shared with others. Generously share your knowledge and experience when an occasion arises. Or take the initiative

and seek out an opportunity. Find a need and meet it. What are some of your talents? How do you utilize your talents? How often do you share them? Who do you share them with? How can you share more of your talents with others?

4. *With your love.* Share your love with others. Be generous with this free yet precious gift. You have the ability to show compassion to others and empathize with their situation. This gift is more valuable than any amount of money. Love will sustain their hearts and let them know they are not alone. It will provide them with strength, hope, and possibly some security. How often do you extend some form of love to others? How can you share love more often? What are some ways to share your love?

5. *With your patience.* When someone is hurting, they may be irrational and, more than likely, emotional. They may say or do things that are illogical and perhaps even hurtful. Be patient with them, understand their stress and confusion, and show them grace. Or, if you are volunteering in a bigger organization or event, be patient if it isn't running as smoothly as you'd like it to. It may be run by others who are also out of their element, volunteering their time and doing their best. Be patient and even flexible, and enjoy the process and fellowship with other well-intentioned people. What are some ways of showing patience toward one another? When did a recent opportunity present itself to you? How did you handle it? What was the circumstance? What did you do well? What would you do differently?

6. *With your acceptance.* Accept where people are in their life journey and who they are. When someone else is hurting, or in need, they are potentially feeling down about their situation and how they arrived there. Accept them as they are and allow them to be themselves as they work through the situation that caused the need. Everyone likes and needs acceptance. Or perhaps it is a business or an organization in need. Also, accept them with their need or desire for help to improve their circumstances or as they continue to

provide for or serve others. How can you be more accepting of others without compromising your values? How do you currently show acceptance to others? What do you do well? Where can you improve?

7. *With your forgiveness.* If warranted, freely extend or accept forgiveness as appropriate. It is a gift that provides freedom from hurt feelings and allows you to move forward peacefully. It is also a gift for the other person, whether they choose to accept it or not. Be generous with forgiveness, especially when it is the right thing to do. How often do you ask for forgiveness? How often do you extend forgiveness to others? Does it come easily to you? How can you be more generous with forgiveness? How do you feel when you either give or receive forgiveness? Why is forgiveness therapeutic? Who benefits from forgiveness?

8. *With your encouragement.* Possibly, all that is needed is encouragement. Offer kind and supportive words or actions to the benefit of the recipient. Find the most critical area of need, focus on love and support, and affirm them. Encourage with any available means, perhaps by sharing advice, hope, and ideas or just listening. How often do you encourage or uplift others? What is holding you back? How can you encourage others throughout your day? Where can you find opportunities? How do you feel when others encourage you?

Benefits of being generous:

- Being filled with joy
- Receiving positive health effects
- Building relationships
- Vibrating positive energy
- Helping others fill a need
- Building character
- Being obedient to the LORD's command
- Spreading the effects to others

When we practice generosity and forgiveness,
we reflect the image of God.
— Mac Canoza

Give more than you take, and you'll
get more than you give.
— Sahil Lavingia

That's what I consider true generosity: You give your
all, and yet you always feel as if it costs you nothing.
— Simone de Beauvoir

You give a little when you give of your possessions.
It is when you give of yourself that you truly give.
— Kahil Gibran

Optimize your generosity. No one on their deathbed
has ever regretted giving too much away.
— Kevin Kelly

The highest-status people in human history are
those who asked for nothing and gave everything.
— Naval Ravikant

 Reflect:

1. Describe what it means to find a need and meet it. How often do you do this? How can you incorporate this mindset more into your life?
2. What does volunteering and serving others mean to you? Is this something you currently do? What are examples of where you could do this? Who benefits from the act of volunteering? Discuss the benefits of volunteering and serving others.

STUDENTS: WHO CONNECTS YOUR DOTS?

3. Name three people you know who volunteer or serve others in some capacity.
4. Describe what this looks like. What character qualities do they possess?
5. Name ten ways you can volunteer to serve others in some manner. How would this positively affect others? How would this affect you? In what ways can you volunteer your time? In what ways can you extend your patience?
6. What does it mean to be generous? What are some benefits of generosity?
7. What did you learn in this chapter that you never thought of before?
8. What other thoughts do you have about serving others, gratitude, and generosity?

CHAPTER 16

Innate Spirituality

The need for a spiritual connection is deeply rooted in the desire to have a personal relationship with God. This connection is essential for overall well-being and a sense of purpose in life. This spiritual connection provides guidance, strength, and comfort in times of need. It also helps provide meaning and direction in life and develops a deeper understanding of faith and beliefs. Each person is created with an innate spirituality and sense of right and wrong, although not everyone pursues the continual development of this. For many, this spiritual connection is the foundation of daily life and is crucial for maintaining a sense of peace, joy, and fulfillment. It also allows the experience of a sense of unity with other believers and the opportunity to actively participate in the faith community. Overall, a spiritual connection is a vital aspect of life, providing a sense of belonging, purpose, and hope.

Where are you spiritually? How have you embraced this innate gift? How have you come to realize the magnitude of the universe and the *impossibility* that it was created out of the *nothingness* of a "big bang"? Only an intelligent Creator could have spoken each magnificent aspect into existence, one day at a time, for six days straight. And then, a day of rest followed. Read Genesis 1: 1 through 2:1-3.

> *In the beginning God created the heavens and the earth. Now the earth was formless and empty, darkness was over the surface of the deep, and the*

STUDENTS: WHO CONNECTS YOUR DOTS?

Spirit of God was hovering over the waters. And God said, "Let there be light," and there was light.
—Genesis 1:1-3 NIV

Look at the evidence down to the smallest cells in the body and the orderliness in which everything was created. Study the Golden Ratio[3] or Fibonacci Sequence[4, 5] to discover every living creature's perfect balance, number, ratio, and sequence. This is not by chance. It is well calculated down to the very last detail. All of life is too complex to be "by chance." Only one who is perfect could have designed all of this. Is it more logical that the complexity of life was created by a perfect, omnipotent God or the *nothingness* of "time" and random "mutations"? What is a mutation anyway? A mutation is a type of *cancer* that destroys rather than allows things to "evolve." The idea of evolution relies on *time* and "by chance" *mutations* to create and change things. How can "time," a nonspatial continuum, and destructive "mutations" create anything? Sit and stare at the air for five, ten, or twenty minutes. What do you notice?

Consider Darwin's theory and the problems with it. His theory says that things evolve by working a little bit, maybe not very well, but a little bit, and then a random mutation occurs—a change comes along that helps it move or work a little bit better—and that helps the organism survive and have more offspring. Then, another random change comes along, and another and another, and that gradually builds up to the final structure. While this might work for some things, it does NOT work for irreducibly complex systems, including things like the microscopic bacterial flagellum. It needs *all* of its current parts to be complete and functional. It would not even function until it has *all* the complete parts. *"With irreducibly complex systems like the flagellum, Darwin's idea is dead in the water, like a boat without an outboard that doesn't work."*[6, 7] Creation all points to an intelligent designer—God. For example, consider a nine-piece simple mouse trap. It takes all nine pieces to be in one exact layout, all accounted for, in order to work. It will not function if this exact sequence isn't in place. More information is found online by searching Michael Behe and the *Irreducible Complexity.*

The "Golden Ratio" is a special name given to describe a ratio that seems to relate indirectly or directly to many aspects of God's creation. The ratio is approximately 1.618. To understand how we observe the ratio of 1.618 in God's creation, we need to look at a special sequence called the Fibonacci numbers.[4, 5] This special sequence begins 0, 1, 1, 2, 3, 5, 8, 13, 21, 34, 55, 89, 144…and continues, with each new number formed by adding the previous two numbers together (1 + 2 = 3, 3 + 5 = 8, etc.) The ratio between most numbers in this sequence is very close to the Golden Ratio. This means that if you divide two neighboring numbers in the Fibonacci Sequence, you will get a number close to 1.618.[3]

Since we find neighboring Fibonacci numbers all over creation, it follows that we also find the Golden Ratio all over, too. For example, the seeds in any given sunflower are arranged in two patterns of spirals. If one of the patterns has 55 spirals, the other will have either 34 or 89—the number of spirals in each pattern is always neighboring numbers in the Fibonacci Sequence. This also means that the ratio between the two patterns is always very close to the Golden Ratio. No matter how large or small the sunflower is, one spiral pattern always contains approximately 1.618 times the number of seeds as the other pattern. This ratio allows for the most number of seeds to fit in any given sunflower.[3]

If you were to look at plants, pinecones, or pineapples, you would again find Fibonacci numbers and the Golden Ratio and be awed again at the Creator. Scientists have even found ways where things like the nautilus' shell relate indirectly to the Golden Ratio. And artists and architects have discovered that rectangles based on the Golden Ratio are artistically pleasing.[3]

Many marvel over how the Golden Ratio (and numbers in the Fibonacci Sequence) keep popping up all over creation. The ratio appears everywhere because God designed the Golden Ratio to have its properties and then designed each part of His creation with infinite care and wisdom, using this ratio to give sunflowers, pinecones, and more just what they needed. He also created your mind to appreciate this same ratio as something "beautiful"—as testified to by the many buildings and paintings that incorporate this ratio.[3]

STUDENTS: WHO CONNECTS YOUR DOTS?

How do you explain all of nature having the same ratio or sequence? What thoughts come to mind? Have you tried the calculation yourself? Where can you find more information regarding this phenomenon? How can you verify the credibility of your resources? Analyze and evaluate this information objectively. What do you notice?

> *The Golden Ratio is a key to understanding the beauty and balance of God's world, from the proportions of a seashell to the petals of a flower.*
> —Jill Fandrich

Consider the majesty of the Grand Canyon. Suppose it had been created slowly over time due to erosion and random "mutations." How could the layers be so perfectly proportioned, containing fossilized *ecosystems* (yes, entire ecosystems are found in specific layers) upon ecosystems, all *equivalent* to other canyons *worldwide?*[8] How is it that fossils of aquatic life are found on *top* of some of the highest mountains? Instead of the slowness of time and cancerous mutations, the canyons resulted from massive amounts of water and catastrophic mudslides, hurricanes, volcanoes, tsunamis, and underground eruptions over a *rapid* period of time. What could explain a quick and catastrophic event in history? When did an occurrence such as this exist? Noah experienced the creation of these canyons at a terrifying pace during the massive flood that covered the entire earth in approximately 2,348 BC. This particular flood is responsible for most of the rock layers and fossils as a result.[8]

Fossilization is *not* a common occurrence. As organic creatures, cells break down over time, such as the decay rate experienced in today's culture. It would take a catastrophic process, such as the incredible powers of moving waters, earthquakes, and volcanic explosions on a colossal scale in a *short* period of time, to fossilize organic creatures and preserve them until the present day. This would unlikely occur simply due to "time" and random and cancerous "mutations." Extensive time would have rotted and broken down bones, and to dust, it would all have returned. So, why are there *fossilized* creatures in a linear fashion worldwide? How is it they are in orderly layers? How do you explain the rapid and simultaneous sedimentation of the Grand Canyon and other canyons around the world?[8]

More informational sources regarding the flood and Creation can be found by searching Ken Ham and Bodie Hodge. Together, they wrote a fascinating series called The Ultimate Answers Pack, including The New Answers Books 1-4 and A Flood of Evidence. They can also be found on YouTube and other internet searches. Ken Ham founded the Creation Museum and the Ark Encounter in Kentucky. There are many other references to explore and apply critical thinking to. Research some or all of these resources.

The Bible is God's written Word divinely inspired through man and is a history of the beginning of our existence as well as a ledger of our future destiny. God communicates to us through His Word and allows us to have a *relationship* with Him. There is a longing or a sense of some kind within us that is hollow and unfulfilled until we choose to fill it with Him. How has this "sense" presented itself in your life? When did you first become aware of it? How did you respond? What are your thoughts regarding it? What questions come to mind? What is your relationship like with your Creator? Do you pray and have a conversation with Him? Do you lean on Him when in need? Do you celebrate with Him when there's a victory? Do you attend Bible-based services or listen to Bible-based podcasts? Do you have a Bible? How often do you read the Bible? Is it a paper version or a digital one? How will you find out more information regarding this topic? What credible sources will you pursue for more information?

God sent His son, Jesus, to earth as a man we can relate to. He "took on flesh," as prophesied in the Bible. His death and resurrection provided us a pathway to one day be reunited with our Creator in the Heavenly realm. The only requirement is to accept Jesus as our Savior, put all our faith in Him, and repent of our sins.

> *For God so loved the world that he gave his one and only Son, that whoever believes in him shall not perish but have eternal life.*
> —John 3:16 NIV

STUDENTS: WHO CONNECTS YOUR DOTS?

Salvation is a gift from God. It does not come by "being a good person" or by works or acts of service performed, lest we brag and are boastful in our own means.

> *For it is by grace you have been saved, through faith—and this is not from yourselves, it is the gift of God—not by works, so that no one can boast.*
> —Ephesians 2:8-9 NIV

Studying the Bible makes it clear that the earth is actually very young! Rather than the evolutionists' guess from the late eighteenth and early nineteenth centuries that the earth is millions or billions of years old, the Bible maps out from the time of Creation to the present day, a matter of about 6,000 – 6,100 years. Follow the genealogy and do your own math.

> *This is the written account of Adam's line. When God created man, he made him in the likeness of God. He created them* male *and* female *and blessed them. And when they were created, he called them "man." When Adam had lived 130 years, he had a son in his own likeness, in his own image; and he named him Seth... Terah became the father of Abram, Nahor and Haran.*
> —Genesis 5:1 through 11:27 NIV

Read from chapter 5 through the end of chapter 11 in Genesis. You will find a genealogy from Adam through Abram, soon to be renamed Abraham. How many years have you calculated so far? The flood occurred about 1,656 years after Creation (~4004 BC to ~2348 BC). Read Genesis chapter 6. The flood to David killing Goliath was ~1,324 years (~2348 BC to ~1024 BC) (1 Samuel 17). David and Goliath to the birth of Jesus add another ~1,019 years (~1024 BC to ~5 BC) (Matthew 1, Mark 1, Luke 2:6, John 1:14). Jesus "took on flesh" and became man a little less than 2,400 years after the catastrophic flood, restarting the calendar at 0, give or take five or six years. Read Matthew 1:1-17, leading from Abraham to the birth of Christ. From the birth of Jesus to 2024 or similar present day is another ~2,029 years, for an approximate total of ~6,000+ years. Calculate for yourself and observe the time you discovered. What have you revealed?

> *A record of the genealogy of Jesus Christ the son of David, the son of Abraham... Thus there were fourteen generations in all from Abraham to David, fourteen from David to the exile to Babylon, and fourteen from the exile to the Christ.*
> —Matthew 1:1-17 NIV

The gospel of Luke also contains a genealogy in reverse. He starts with Jesus and names the ancestors all the way back to Adam. Read Luke 3:23-38. The book of Ruth lists the genealogy of David. Read Ruth 4:13-22. What do you notice?

And here you are, roughly 2000+ years after the birth of Jesus Christ. In case you are unaware, the date acknowledged as our current time indicator here in the 21st century is derived from the approximate number of years since Jesus Christ was born. That totals almost 6,100 years since Creation.

Everyone is created in the image of God, and there lies the innate sense of a spiritual being He created within us. Have you connected spiritually with God the Father? What is your current connection? Are you fulfilled? Are you holding back? If so, what is holding you back? Take some time to research and seek God. Pray for discernment and guidance. What do you have to lose? What might you have to gain? Is it worth risking an eternity in a fiery, painful realm, empty, desolate, and alone? If you believe there is even the slightest chance that God is calling you to a relationship with Him, what do you have to lose? Imagine an eternity in paradise, filled with constant love, joy, and a complete relationship with your Creator. What might the consequences be of disregarding this relationship? What might they be for pursuing it? Discuss the pros and cons of each. Where does free will fall into place? Discuss free will.

STUDENTS: WHO CONNECTS YOUR DOTS?

God wants a relationship with you, but He did give you free will. He will not force you. No matter what you may have done or think you have done, He loves you and wants a relationship with you. What are your thoughts regarding this relationship? How can you take advantage of this free gift? Identify any obstacles that may be holding you back. Will you take the step to acknowledge yourself as a sinner, repent, and recognize Christ as your Savior?

> *Above all, you must understand that in the last days scoffers will come, scoffing and following their own evil desires. They will say, "Where is this 'coming' he promised? Ever since our ancestors died, everything goes on as it has since the beginning of creation." But they deliberately forget that long ago by God's word the heavens came into being and the earth was formed out of water and by water. By these waters also the world of that time was deluged and destroyed. By the same word the present heavens and earth are reserved for fire, being kept for the day of judgment and destruction of the ungodly.*
> —2 Peter 3:3-7 NIV

 Reflect:

1. What are your thoughts about being born with an innate sense of right and wrong? How readily do you listen to your "conscience"?
2. Describe where you are spiritually. Do you lean on God when you need strength? Have you accepted Christ as your Savior?
3. Name three people you know who have a strong relationship with God. Describe what this looks like.

4. Read the previously mentioned Bible passages and calculate the time span of the earth. What have you discovered? Watch the YouTube video referenced at the back of the book *Is Genesis History?*⁶ Discuss your thoughts regarding the video.
5. When experiencing a difficult time, who do you rely on? Why did you choose this person or persons? Do you turn to God for His guidance and support? How can you place your faith in God's loving hands? How do you "give it to God"?
6. When experiencing an exciting event, do you thank God and recognize His provisions? How can you incorporate this more into your day?
7. When you do something well or accomplish something, do you take full credit or acknowledge God's allowance of your gifts?
8. Research the Creation Museum and the Ark Encounter. What have you learned?
9. What other thoughts do you have about spirituality and your relationship with God?

CHAPTER 17

Leadership Skills

Character qualities and leadership skills are crucial in determining a person's success. While numerous attributes contribute to success, certain qualities are essential in driving effective leadership and achieving personal and professional goals. Incorporating these qualities and skills into your programming is instrumental in paving the path to success.

Developing character qualities is important for several reasons:

1. *Personal growth* - Developing strong character qualities such as honesty, integrity, and responsibility can lead to personal growth and self-improvement. These qualities help you build better character traits and navigate through life with a sense of purpose and direction. Define honesty. What does this look like? How important is honesty in all of your interactions? How about your schoolwork? What is integrity? How do you display integrity? Why is it an important personal and professional quality? Are you a responsible person? Do you take responsibility for your actions—*all* of them? How do you show responsibility in your schoolwork?
2. *Building positive relationships* - Character qualities such as empathy, kindness, and respect are essential for building strong and positive relationships with others. These qualities can help you communicate effectively, resolve conflicts, and create meaningful connections with others.

How can you be empathetic about another person's suffering or failure? What does empathy look like? How is this quality important for strong relationships? How do you develop it? How can you show kindness, as described in chapter 11? What are the characteristics of it? How do you show respect for others? In what ways can you respect your parents, other students, teachers, and professors?

3. *Leadership and success* - Developing character qualities such as determination, perseverance, and resilience are crucial for success and leadership. These qualities can help you overcome challenges, set and achieve goals, and inspire and lead others. How determined are you when you set your mind on something? How can determination turn a challenge into a success? How do you gain more determination? Describe what it means to persevere. Give examples of how you persevered during a challenging time. How did you do this? What did it take to persevere? What is resilience? In what ways can resilience lead to successful results? How can you become resilient?

4. *Contributing to society* - Character qualities such as compassion, generosity, and empathy are essential for positively contributing to society. These qualities can motivate you to help others, volunteer, and make a difference in your community. How compassionate are you? How can compassion help build better relationships? How can you gain more compassion for others? How generous are you? Generosity involves more than just a financial offering. In what ways can you be generous?

5. *Moral and ethical values* - Character qualities are also important for shaping moral and ethical values. Developing strong character qualities can help you make sound decisions and act in a way that is ethical and just. How do you ensure your choices are aligned with your values? Have you taken the time to outline, list, or in some way define your values? What are some consequences of making decisions against your values? How could this affect you, your family, or others you love?

STUDENTS: WHO CONNECTS YOUR DOTS?

Character development is important for personal growth, building positive relationships, success and leadership, contributing to society, and shaping moral and ethical values. It ultimately leads to a more fulfilling and meaningful life. Character qualities are essential for leadership and professional growth as well.

Along with continually building your character, there are other leadership skills you can develop. For example, how do you approach a simple, daily, typical task? How do you proceed toward a daunting task? How do you respond to an unexpected obstacle? Most often, the outcomes of your circumstances are directly linked to the demeanor of the approach taken as you engage in numerous scenarios. How do you develop a creative and innovative mind? How do you learn to explore different problem-solving methods before making a final decision?

Your attitude is infectious and carries over into how you process information and respond or react. Think about a time when you received some sort of good news or joy and how this emotion carried with you into projects, decisions, conversations, or even thoughts following the event. Do you remember how open and free-flowing your mind was during this time? Your thoughts were probably bursting with innovative and creative abundance, desperate for a problem to solve! Now, think of an event that led to intense feelings of stress, pain, or negativity, and recall the tightness in your mind and the squashing of thoughts, ideas, and solutions. It was probably a struggle to think rationally or make the simplest decisions. Do you recall your productivity level following these harsh and adverse emotions? In each scenario, recall how you felt and responded in both a personal and professional aspect. Do you wish you would have responded or handled yourself differently? Would you like to acclimate yourself to a new automatic response for future situations? Reframe your mind with a positive approach.

Benefits of choosing a positive approach:

1. *Your mind expands.* When you allow positive energy to flow through your body's cells, your mind expands and is open to ideas, possibilities, new thoughts, creative alternatives,

and a realization of an abundance of opportunities and solutions. It is endless where your mind will take you when it flows with high-frequency vibrations, and it expands and gives way to even more good thoughts and ideas in return. And where your focus goes, energy flows, and actions show. And in this case, positive and favorable actions will result. How can you expand your mind with favorable thoughts? How would this affect other areas in your life? How can you turn negative thoughts into positive ones?

2. *Avoidance of mental clutter.* Encountering events with a positive attitude prevents stress and anxiety from accumulating and cluttering your mind. When you allow negativity to build up and block the free flow of light and easy thoughts, the negative, heavier ones layer upon themselves and build up clutter in your mind—think of them as "sticky" and heavy. Once they build up, it is difficult to remove them, and any light favorable thought could get trapped or "stuck" to the clutter, accumulating and breeding more negativism or stress, thereby losing its initial impact. Choosing a positive approach each time can prevent the buildup or layering of this tacky, unwanted, heavy thought process. How much mental clutter has your mind accumulated? How do you currently address it? What are other ways you can think of to remove the clutter?

3. *Building confidence in yourself.* As you begin each endeavor with a positive outlook, and your mind and thoughts respond with an abundance of creative ideas for pursuit, you will build confidence in yourself and your ability to not only handle any situation but also to handle it well, with wisdom, creativity, grace, and ultimately, success. A positive approach is a sure sign of a confident person. How confident are you? Where does your confidence come from? Are you confident with your confidence? How can you gain more? How would you benefit from more?

4. *Building respect and confidence from others.* With a consistently positive approach, others will perceive you as a

STUDENTS: WHO CONNECTS YOUR DOTS?

person who is confident, capable, and responsible enough to handle random conditions that present themselves at any time, and you possess the ability to keep a level head with the determination to persevere. People will trust your leadership and decision-making abilities. How are others affected by your approach? Is your approach generally positive or negative? When you display positivity, how do others respond to you? Which way draws the best response? What are you doing well? What changes can you make to improve your approach?

5. *Improved quality of life.* Leading your life with a positive approach will guarantee a more peaceful and enjoyable quality of life. Challenges will always be expected at some point, and often many, but a positive outlook allows for a spirit of peace and contentment and a sense of security that there will always be a variety of solutions, willing people to help, and wisdom and serenity that flows through an open mind. How could your life be improved with a more positive attitude? What changes need to be made? How could this impact your life? In what ways would it be affected? Where would be a good place to begin?

6. *A leader to be imitated.* When you approach your life with a commendatory pursuit, you will be exemplified by those seeking to acquire the leadership skills you are displaying. It is not always easy to choose to see obstacles with a hope-filled favorable approach and underlying security that a solution will soon be uncovered. It is even unnatural. That is why it will cause you to shine as a leader above the many. This outstanding character quality will refine your image and induce the reputation of an admirable leader. How can you stand out as a leader among others? How would you currently rate your ability to lead? How could a positive approach draw others to follow your lead?

7. *You are approachable.* If you think about someone negatively approaching a task, it is difficult to muster the strength to want to become part of the solution by

working alongside this person. When you have a pleasant and hopeful demeanor, you indirectly encourage others to open their minds to possible creative ideas and solutions and instigate the desire to engage in the process. People each have their own distinct experiences and can each draw on different situations. This is very advantageous and opens doors to various possible solutions or outcomes. Let the positive energy flow throughout each situation and person encountered, and be amazed at the propensity of possibilities. Why are people drawn to other positive people? How would this benefit both you and them? What are the possible benefits? How can being positively approachable increase your likelihood of success?

It is common sense to reason that high importance should be placed on how you approach things in your life. As your responses to situations are basically preprogrammed, based on how you already trained your mind to process information and then react, it is worthwhile to evaluate the *source* of your thoughts and your current state of mind. Is it filled with positive high-frequency vibrations? Or is it filled with negative clutter? As discussed previously, if your mind is filled with heavy, low-density mental clutter, it blocks the flow of ideas, creativity, and solutions. Although it will take time, breaking down and eliminating this clutter and replacing and filling your mind with positive energy, thoughts, and ideas is vital and worthwhile. When your mind is conditioned in this supportive manner, your approach, responses, and outcomes to situations will already be preprogrammed to be light, favorable, creative, fruitful, and abundantly advantageous.

Some ideas for clearing clutter include recognizing the derivation of the negative source or sources, utilizing mindful awareness, and then choosing to release the negativity. Meditation and prayer are beneficial to clearing and reframing the mind with favorable, positive, and promising thoughts, ideas, and concepts. A healthy diet, proper nutrition, and some form of exercise will also aid in feelings of well-being and overall health and wellness. Plenty of sleep is also imperative to this healthy process. The key is to focus on prioritizing this and finding what works best for you to reprogram your mind from a form of negativism to a state of positive energy and experience the affirmative and constructive qualities that go hand-in-hand with it. Keep in mind that it takes many weeks to form an actual "habit." With consistency, decluttering your mind and reframing it with positive, favorable thoughts can actually become an automatic response. It is all a choice only you can make, and it is *positively* astounding and endlessly worthwhile.

A leadership skill that is worth taking the time to develop is the ability to turn a negative into a positive. As you have undoubtedly already heard, failure is simply one of many ways NOT to do something. And it isn't actually "failure" unless you quit trying. Before the very moment of a decision to quit, it is still part of the pathway to success. Success is the result of a long process that takes diligent and consistent effort in order to attain. Lots of perseverance and hard work are involved. But it can be such an exciting and stimulating process! It is the journey that matters.

There is so much to be learned, and new information is amazing! It leads to "new-merous" ideas and different ways of doing things. An array of differing opportunities is bound to arise with various possible outcomes. It is a perfect time to open your mind and grow from the priceless knowledge revealed. Observe what did not go the way you desired and seek out why. Could that be an opportunity in itself to pursue a different direction? Or is it knowledge of something to eliminate from the original pathway you are striving for? Take time to learn from this result. What new choices will you make as a result of it? What five things come to mind as you observe the process that led to this outcome? What will you alter as you continue in pursuit of your desired goal? How can this new information help you travel down an even more advantageous pathway?

Information is priceless. This step has given you more information to be used for an even better future outcome. Do not allow negative thoughts to cloud or hinder your goals. Do not allow this to change your goals unless you are even more motivated to enhance them further, especially knowing you are aware of an additional way not to do things. Allow yourself to raise your energy to positive, high-frequency vibrations. Clear your mind of all negative thoughts. And when you have taken the time to do this, come to the realization that "not succeeding" the first time in something has many benefits.

Benefits of not succeeding the first time:

1. *Knowledge of what not to do.* When you know what not to do, your mind opens to selecting more appropriate things you can try next.
2. *Confidence and relief.* Knowing what not to do makes you more confident that you are getting closer to your target or goal. In addition, you should feel relief that the unfavorable outcome occurred when it did so it can be resolved early in the goal development.
3. *Motivation.* Discovering an obstacle while reaching for your goals places you one step closer to those goals. This can build motivation and positive energy as you wade through the process of elimination.
4. *Innovation.* With your new knowledge, your mind can expand, let positive energy flow through it, and raise your vibrations, allowing innovative, creative ideas to flow. Take full advantage of this outpouring of thoughts and give them the freedom to take you to uncharted territory.
5. *Perseverance.* Rather than allow a setback to slow you down, reverse the idea, see it as a "move forward," and be determined to see your goals reach fruition.
6. *Pride.* The good kind. Take pride in the fact that you are moving toward the goals you have set for yourself. Be proud of yourself for working hard and persevering in search of a favorable way to reach the desired outcome.
7. *Joy and contentment.* Allow yourself to enjoy the journey! Consider it all joy as you learn, grow, discover, and recreate.

STUDENTS: WHO CONNECTS YOUR DOTS?

Be sure *not* to lower your goal when you experience a "move forward." Never decrease your goal. Rather, *step up your action!* This alone will separate you from others. People are often inclined to lower their goals in order to reach them. Instead, lead the way as you double, triple, or even quadruple your actions. Try more ideas, give more thought, study harder, make more effort, place more calls, and do more research. *Take more action!* Make your effort in abundance, and never give up. Stay focused on your goals and give them full attention. Where your attention goes, energy flows, and actions show.

> *You will never fail unless you give up.*
> *And giving up is not an option.*
> —Jill Fandrich

> *Success is measured by how high you*
> *bounce when you hit bottom.*
> —George S. Patton

> *The Phoenix must burn to emerge.*
> —Janet Fitch

Effective leadership is shaped by starting with a "beginner's mind." A beginner's mind is the perfect place to build essential leadership and critical thinking skills to foster innovative thinking and problem-solving skills found in leaders. The first step is to declutter the mind and discover where all of the current thought processes are coming from. Bring yourself to an awareness of your current programming and observe your current reactions, responses, and results. Are you where you want to be? Program your mind for successful thinking by filling it with character qualities, positive thinking and mind programming, and effective leadership skills.

 Reflect:

1. Name as many character qualities as you can think of. How are these effective for personal and professional growth?
2. Which of these qualities do you exemplify most? Which ones do you still need to incorporate into your programming?
3. Name three people you know who display numerous character qualities.
4. Describe what this looks like. Which qualities are they? How have these qualities defined them as a successful person?
5. Think of a time when there was an event or situation, and you approached it negatively. What was the outcome? How can you reframe this situation with a positive approach? Describe what that would look like. How do you think the outcome would differ?
6. Name a failure in your past. How can you reframe it into a success? How will you adjust your mindset to look at future failures positively?
7. What other thoughts do you have about character qualities and other leadership skills?

CHAPTER 18

Finances

How do you view finances? Are you responsible with them? Do you currently have a job? Do you have a bank account or financial App? Are you familiar with how to write out a check? How do you deposit a check? How do you use a debit card or ATM (automated teller machine)? How about the chip technology in the cards? How do you use Apple Pay? Do you use regular paper money or coin cash? How many other forms of payment can you think of? What is your favorite form of digital payment? What form of payment do you use the most? Where can you find out more information about how to use different forms of payment and the various methods of use? Become comfortable with different options, so you are ready for various circumstances. Yet, still be cautious of sneaky hackers and their ability to either scam you or invade your finances. Think critically about what might be the best form for your circumstances.

How do you manage your money? How do you prioritize money management? What source or sources do you use for help? There are many credible and excellent resources for learning money management tips and strategies to choose from. The one selected for this chapter for the sake of discussion is by Dave Ramsey. Dave Ramsey has put together a helpful program about handling money and establishing a budget known as *Financial Peace University*.[9] This course is an ultimate information source for successful, as well as biblical, money management. *Financial Peace University* is a nine-week class that teaches you the step-by-step plan to win with money and gives you all the tools you need to work it. Many free resources may be accessed on the website ramseysolutions.com. As always, ask CT questions when you select your own money management method and budgeting tools.

Financial Peace University includes:

1. Baby Step 1 (Save $1,000 for your starter emergency fund) & Budgeting
2. Baby Step 2 (Pay off all debt—except a house—using the debt snowball)
3. Baby Step 3 (Save 3-6 months of expenses in a fully funded emergency fund)
4. Baby Steps 4, 5, 6, & 7 (4—Invest 15% of your household income in retirement, 5—Save for a college fund, 6—Pay off your home early, 7—Build wealth and give)
5. Wise Spending
6. Understanding Insurance
7. Building Wealth
8. Buying & Selling Your Home
9. Outrageous Generosity

How do you currently handle money? Have you experienced debt? What credible sources can you research on methods of staying out of debt in the first place? What value results from debt avoidance? Consider researching an average house cost and an average loan. Calculate the interest amount resulting from a 15-year and a 30-year fixed loan. Compare the differences in payments and fees involved. How do you feel about losing that much money in interest fees? What are the differences between these two options? What other options for home ownership or living scenarios are available?

What do you know about debt? How could this affect your ability to maintain your current or desired lifestyle? How would this affect your ability to "get ahead" in life? What does "getting ahead" look like to you? Whether you're trying to get out of debt, save for a fun purchase, or save for retirement, you'll learn God's way of handling money through Dave Ramsey's program. No matter where you are in your financial journey, a financial program or plan such as *Financial Peace University* helps you reach your goals faster. What are your financial goals? Where do you want to be financially five years from now? Ten years? Twenty years? What is your plan for getting there? The sooner you start asking yourself these questions and devising a plan, the more financially sound your future will be.

Now for the dreaded B-word—*budgeting*. Unfortunately, the word budget has gotten a bad rap. But when it all boils down, a budget is just a *plan for your money*. No matter what you've heard or thought about budgeting in the past, hear this: A budget doesn't limit your freedom—*it gives you freedom*! It's literally you taking control, getting intentional, and telling your money where it will go with every single dollar you make.

Have you ever practiced budgeting before? Have you saved your own money for a bicycle, cellphone, AirPods, laptop, or other item of interest? How did you determine what you needed to do to make the numbers work out? What credible sources did you use? How did you plan for this to occur? Did you create a timeline for purchase? Whether you are just getting started in the budgeting world or want to prepare for your future, these budgeting tips will help.

Fifteen budgeting tips:

1. *Budget to zero before the month begins.* This means before the month even starts, you're making a plan and giving *every* dollar a name. This is what is called a *zero-based budget*. That doesn't mean you have zero dollars in your bank account. (Leave a buffer of extra money when possible.) It just means your income minus all your expenses equals zero. This is how you make sure none of your money slips through the cracks or gets spent by accident. Take full control of every dollar you make.

2. *Do the budget together.* You need a financial accountability partner. Find someone who will encourage you—*and* help you stick to your goals. Have a monthly budget meeting to review what happened last month and what's coming up. Make it fun! Grab some of your favorite snacks and put on a good playlist. You need to get on the same page with money, so set goals together and dream about what the future will look like.

3. *Remember that every month is different.* Some months, you will have to budget for certain things, such as necessities or routine car maintenance, if you own your own car. You will save for fun things like electronics, vacations, birthdays, and holidays in other months. Ensure you prepare for all your expenses—even those not-so-fun ones. Keep those special occasions from sneaking up on you by pulling up your calendar while creating your budget.

4. *Start with the most important categories first.* Giving and saving are at the top of the list, and then comes the Four Walls: food, utilities, shelter, and transportation. Not all of these categories may apply to a student, but it is good to be aware of them now to prepare for your future. You may need to substitute different categories for now. Once your true necessities are taken care of, you can fill in the rest of the categories in your budget.

5. *Pay off your debt.* If you have debt, paying it off must be a top priority in your budget. Use the *debt snowball method* and the *7 Baby Steps* described on Dave's website to get rid of debt as quickly as possible. Attack it! Get mad at it! Stop letting debt rob you of the very thing that helps you win with money—your income. When you stop paying for the past, you can start truly budgeting for the present—and the future!

6. *Don't be afraid to trim the budget.* Brace yourself! It might be time for some budget cuts in your life. If things are tight right now because of inflation, a low-paying job,

STUDENTS: WHO CONNECTS YOUR DOTS?

inconsistent hours, having limited time to work due to school, or whatever reason, you can save money quicker by trimming your budget. Find ways to trim spending or to make more money. Remember, your budget cuts don't have to last forever. You can always make adjustments later on.

7. *Set auto drafts where possible.* Paying bills isn't the most exciting part of life, especially in your adult life. But it's also unavoidable. Save time and stress by setting up auto drafts for a few of your bills when you can. Just make sure you're paying attention to your cash flow. If you set up too many auto drafts <u>and</u> spend more than normal, you might end up over-drafting your account. Know when the money's coming in and out of your bank account!

8. *Have goals.* Whether you're paying off student loans, building an emergency fund, or paying off another debt, you must focus on your *why*. Why are you making these sacrifices? Use your <u>why</u> to set goals that get you closer to the life you are dreaming of. Then, write down your goals. Make them visible. And give them a timeline so you're always making progress. Remember your <u>why</u> and keep your goals in front of you. This will help you stay motivated even when you don't feel like budgeting.

9. *Track your progress.* Speaking of goals, don't set them up and forget about them. Keep tracking your progress. Those monthly budget meetings are a perfect time to talk about your goals. Celebrate how far you've come and spend time looking at what's left to tackle. Get real with yourself. Is your current budget helping you move forward? If your spending habits don't align with your goals, think about how to cut expenses or increase your income so you can reach your dreams faster.

10. *Keep a miscellaneous line in your budget.* Here's a budgeting tip you can start this minute: Put a small amount of money aside for unexpected monthly expenses. Label this as your miscellaneous line in your budget. That way, when

something comes up, you can cover it without taking away money you've already put elsewhere. If the same specific expenses keep popping up in this category, it's probably time to give them their own budget line.

11. *Cut up your credit cards.* Not only do you need to pay off debt, but you also need to ditch those credit cards for good if you have any. Stop using them! Cut them up, shred them, or even make a craft project out of them! Whatever you do, get the temptation of more debt out of your life. People often say they pay off the balance at the end of the month, but even if that's you, making one lump payment monthly is a horrible money management system. You don't know where your money's truly going, so you can never fully take control of it. You may be racking up interest, and your income is literally stuck in the past. Instead, get ahead with your money; that's what these budgeting tips are all about. Stick to using your debit card or cash, and dump the credit cards.

12. *Use cash for certain budget categories that trip you up.* If you are constantly overspending on a particular item or fun purchases, cash out those categories and use the *envelope system* to hold you accountable. Go to the bank and pull out the cash you've budgeted for that category. Once the cash runs out, stop spending! It's the ultimate accountability partner.

13. *Try an online budget tool.* If pen and paper (or spreadsheets) aren't your thing, it's time to join the 21st century and use a budgeting tool like *EveryDollar.* You can focus on planning a budget and tracking your spending from the comfort of your smartphone. Plus, you can sync up your budget with your accountability partner, which keeps that communication open. There are many different tools to choose from.

14. *Be content and quit the comparisons.* You have much more than you realize. Don't compare your situation to anyone

else's. Comparison will rob you of not only your joy but also your paycheck. Keep moving forward and doing what's right for <u>your</u> paycheck, goals, and life.

15. *Give yourself lots of grace.* One of the key things to remember about budgeting is this: It usually takes three to four months to get a handle on it. Your budget won't be perfect the first time or the second. But you'll get there. So give yourself some grace as you go. Learn from your mistakes—and keep pushing forward.

How to make a budget:
Here are five steps to make a budget:

Budget Step 1: List your income.

Start by listing the money you plan on getting during that month: normal paychecks and anything extra from a garage sale, gifts, a freelance job, or a side hustle.

Budget Step 2: List your expenses.

Next, list your expenses, starting with giving/tithing, saving, and the *Four Walls* discussed previously, such as food, utilities, shelter, transportation, or whatever categories apply to you today. Then, list all the other monthly expenses, starting with essentials and ending with fun stuff. This includes debt, insurance, savings, entertainment, and any personal spending.

Budget Step 3: Subtract your expenses from your income.

According to the zero-based budget mentioned earlier, subtracting your expenses from your income should equal zero. What happens if you do that math and have extra left over? Don't just leave it, or you'll impulse spend it here and there without even thinking. Give it a job by putting it toward the *Baby Step* you're on. What if you get a negative number? Hey—it'll be okay. But you must cut back on the extras or pick up extra work to cover it. Don't skip this essential budgeting tip: Put any extra money you make to work. Get it in the budget.

EveryDollar and other budgeting apps or tools will do all the math for you.

Budget Step 4: Track your transactions.

The way you'll win with budgeting is to track your transactions. That means you put every expense and every bit of income into your budget all month long. This helps you stay accountable to yourself, your accountability partner, and your money. You aren't hiding spending from anyone. And you won't overspend because you'll know what's left in every budget line.

Budget Step 5: Make a new budget before the month begins.

When you budget before the month begins, you prepare for everything coming your way. Do not skip this step: Make a new budget—every single month.

Budgeting Tip for Inconsistent or Irregular Income:

If you have an inconsistent or irregular income, you can still budget. As you list your income, go with what a low-earning month would look like for you. Then, as you are listing expenses, prioritize needs before wants. If your income ends up being more than you planned, you can add money toward your current *Baby Step* or one of those extras you skipped when you first set the budget.

STUDENTS: WHO CONNECTS YOUR DOTS?

How Can Budgeting Help You?

There are many ways a budget can help you. Here are a few:

- A budget shows you—with 100% clarity—exactly where your money's going, so there's no more wondering where you spent it each month.
- Budgeting makes you feel like you got a raise. The average *EveryDollar* user says they find extra money in their first month using this budgeting tool. That money was spent on who knows what before—but now *you* get to decide where it goes.
- If you're the type who feels bad when you spend money, you can shop without guilt, knowing that expense is already in the budget. You're just following the plan.
- No matter what money goal you're working on—getting out of debt, saving for retirement, saving for a vacation, or just trying to keep your fun-spending bill from getting out of hand—budgeting is how you get there.

How Can You Make a Budget Quickly?

The quickest way to set up (and stick to) a budget is by using a free budgeting tool such as *EveryDollar*. Many other options are available and are currently in the App Store or even through an online scan. With these tools, you can quickly map out next month's budget and keep up with it easily. When you realize the purpose of budgeting isn't to limit your freedom but to *give* you freedom, you'll be on the road to loving your life and bank account.

How have you been handling your finances? How important is it to gain an understanding of money management? Where can you find more information? Have you ever experienced debt before? If so, how do you feel about it? What steps will you take to work your way out of it? How can debt be dangerous? What are ways you can avoid future debt? What steps will you take to avoid debt? Have you ever budgeted before? How can budgeting help in preventing debt? What are the other benefits of budgeting? How many budgeting tools can you find? What is your favorite one? How will you use budgeting to save for your future? Think critically when it comes to your finances. What other money management ideas can you research?

 Reflect:

1. List your financial goals for the following year in detail. What are your specific short-term financial goals? Mid-term? Long-term financial goals?
2. Describe how you will measure your financial goals. Include a detailed plan.
3. Give yourself a reasonable yet challenging deadline for each goal.
4. Create a method in which you will sustain these goals. Start a binder, maintain a notebook, or create a Word document on a computer. Goals are more achievable when they are in writing. Review this list daily or weekly. Establish a routine.
5. Share your goals with at least one other person and establish accountability with this person.
6. Name three resources you will refer to for more information about finances, budgeting, and money management.
7. Research and select your favorite budgeting tool and begin budgeting your money.
8. How can you critically think about finances? What questions do you have? Where can you find credible resources for answers?

CHAPTER 19

College and Careers

Reaching a decision about college and a career is a big responsibility. It takes a lot of thought-filled processing with much consideration. What are your current thoughts about college and careers? What fields do you find the most intriguing? What can you see yourself doing as a future career? What kind and how much training is involved to attain the proper education for this field? How can you learn more about this field and the training required? How much does it cost to attain an education in this field? How many years of training are involved? Are there additional opportunities for advanced positions? What type of salary can be made? Will this sustain your desired quality of life? Where is the training provided? Is it close to home, or is there extensive travel involved?

There is a lot to consider when selecting a future career. It is important to consider many options for a future career choice. Find something you can imagine yourself doing for dozens of years. You can always make a career change, but begin your search with thoughts of longevity in your chosen field. What things matter to you the most in a career? What matters the least? What things really don't matter at all? What skills will you need? How will you be able to attain them? At what cost can this occur? What sacrifices will need to be made? Are you willing to make them?

Some things to consider when choosing a career:

1. *Self-assessment.* What are your skills, interests, values, and personality? What activities and subjects do you enjoy? Which ones do you excel in? The most successful career choice will be one that is aligned with your strengths and passions.
2. *Research.* What options are available? What aligns closely with your skills and interests? Is there a demand for any of them currently? What is the job outlook, salary potential, required education, and potential for growth in this field?
3. *Seek advice.* What mentors, career counselors, and professionals can you talk to in the fields you are interested in? Where else can you find valuable insights and advice based on experiences?
4. *Gain experience.* Where can you participate in an internship, part-time job, or volunteer in the fields that interest you? This will help you gain practical experience and determine if the career is a good fit for you.
5. *Set goals.* Set achievable and realistic goals once you have a few potential career paths in mind. How can you gain specific skills, a certain degree, or network with professionals in the industry?
6. *Continued learning.* How can you keep learning and updating your skills to stay competitive in your chosen field? Where can you take advantage of training programs, workshops, or continuing education opportunities?

Remember that choosing a career is not always a linear path, and making changes along the way is okay. The key is being open to new opportunities and continuously evaluating and adapting to your changing interests and goals.

STUDENTS: WHO CONNECTS YOUR DOTS?

Some things to consider regarding college:

1. *What are your career goals?* What are your specific professional desires and milestones you aspire to reach? Do you desire to advance to a certain position, attain a specific title, or earn a monetized salary? Will a specific skill set be required? How can you stay motivated and focused on achieving these goals? Have you set realistic yet challenging goals?

2. *What are your financial considerations?* Research all costs, including tuition, living expenses, textbooks, supplies, equipment fees, and potential student loan debt. How will you handle room and board? Would you choose to live on or off campus? How would transportation be affected or provided? How about commuting to and from home on breaks and holidays? Would financial aid be applied for? What about grants or loans? What are the short-term and long-term financial implications of attending college? What is the cost of living in the college town or city? How would expenses be managed while at college? Who would manage expenses while at college? Would you work at the same time? What options are there for employment while attending classes?

3. *What is your readiness?* Are you ready for the academic and social challenges of college life? How would you organize your time? Are you able to take the initiative to attend all classes and get up on time? How will you develop self-discipline? Will you tackle your own cooking, laundry, and personal finances? How will you organize deadlines, important dates, and commitments? Are you prepared to take effective notes and seek support when needed?

4. *What are the options?* What is the availability of alternative educational or vocational paths, such as trade schools or apprenticeships? What trades are currently in demand? What trade schools are available in your area? Do any of

them interest you? What is the cost of them compared to college? Do any involve apprenticeships and on-the-job training?

5. *What are the potential benefits of college?* How will you gain by earning a college degree in terms of employment opportunities and earning potential? Will you have expanded growth and earning opportunities? Will you benefit from a broader range of subjects and career choices? How will you benefit from experiencing college life? How will this affect your personal growth? How will you be affected socially? What other considerations come to mind? How can networking be affected? How could this affect your personal growth and development of lifelong learning habits?

6. *What are the lifestyle and networking opportunities available?* Attending college offers a new experience of social networking and independence. What different types of fitness and wellness opportunities might be available? How could social clubs and organizations affect your development? Joining groups could provide opportunities to connect with like-minded individuals and build friendships. What other lifestyle and networking opportunities could be available within the surrounding community or on campus?

7. *What other aspects of college life are involved?* Personal interests and passions may be further explored and developed in a college setting. Many towns and cities host events and festivals that may entail a new experience or different theme than you've previously experienced.

8. *What are your family's expectations?* Are there any family expectations for pursuing a college education that must be considered? How do your parents or guardians feel about college decisions? How much input do they contribute to your decision? What explanations or reasons are they providing? Consider all of the information provided with an open mind.

9. *What would be the impact of delaying college?* How might delaying or forgoing college impact future career prospects and goals? Delaying college could have both positive and negative impacts. It could provide an opportunity to save money, gain work experience, travel, or pursue other personal interests, leading to greater maturity and a clearer direction. However, it could mean missing out on the traditional college experience, including building relationships, participating in campus activities, and gaining access to academic and career development resources. It could also delay future job opportunities and earning potential.

10. *What does the college stand for?* Be sure you do extensive research into the colleges you are considering. Many colleges now have a sociopolitical agenda and are more focused on forcing their agenda of manipulative content onto eager students rather than objectively teaching educational content. Where can you find information on the curriculum? How will you verify the credibility of the content? Do your own research and ensure your choices align with your values.

11. *What are the pros and cons?* What are your individual strengths and weaknesses regarding academic readiness and motivation for higher education? List the pros and cons of college, considering all of the previously discussed information.

Considering college and a career involves reflecting on your interests, strengths, values, and goals to make informed decisions about future education and employment. It requires CT, researching different colleges and degree programs, and exploring various career options and job markets. Additionally, it involves considering the financial aspects of higher education and the potential return on investment in terms of future earnings and job satisfaction. Ultimately, considering college and a career is about setting yourself up for a successful and fulfilling future. What other thoughts come to mind regarding college and future careers?

 **Reflect:**

1. What are your current thoughts about college? Explain.
2. What are your current thoughts about a career? What are your five most passionate interests?
3. List five pros and five cons of college.
4. What type of lifestyle will your career need to fund? What will it take to reach these lifestyle goals?
5. What concerns do you have about your future college or career decision?
6. What financial concerns do you have about these topics? What ideas do you have as a resolution?
7. When you think about college and careers, what excites you the most? Why? What concerns you the most? Why?
8. What resources are available for more information on college and career decisions?

CHAPTER 20

Why All the Propaganda?

What is the purpose of propaganda, and where did it all begin? Propaganda has become a powerful tool used to gain approval. It is a way to sway the masses through all available media sources by those in a position to do so, including the military! While the origins, or its inception, were innocent enough in 1622, according to Edward Bernays in his book *Propaganda*, it has now evolved into an entity of "troubling connotation" as it has become a method of *manipulation* and intended enterprise.[10] Propaganda is used today as a method of *controlling* how *you* think and act.

In 2013, the President of the United States signed the Smith-Mundt Modernization Act of 2012 into law, which was part of the 2013 National Defense Authorization Act, which essentially *legalized lying* to the public for propaganda purposes.[11] *"Today, the military is more focused on manipulating news and commentary on the internet, especially social media, by posting material and images without necessarily claiming ownership."* News and journalist reporting are *no longer required* to be factual. This is all befitting George Orwell's literary work, *Nineteen Eighty-Four*.[12] The American people are now being propagandized by the U.S. government through many forms, including via control of major media outlets, Big Pharma, social media, and the tech giants, to name a few. Take some time to read sources such as *Propaganda, Nineteen Eighty-Four, Animal Farm, United States of Fear,* the Smith-Mundt Modernization Act, *Turtles All The Way Down,*[13, 14] and many other sources of your own choosing.

While you may have already noticed the media not relaying factual content, were you aware that they have been given *permission*, and have even been encouraged, to *deliberately deceive* you? Apply CT methods to this topic. Who is involved in the deception? What is the agenda of the deception? Who will benefit from the deception? What are the underlying reasons for the deception? Why would a law have been passed to allow government sources to lie to the American people? What would their perspective potentially be regarding this topic? Do they have *your* best interests in mind? What is your perspective on this topic? What is your response to the permission to deceive in order to persuade you? How does this affect you? How will this configure your thoughts as you listen to the media outlets from now on? Will you apply CT questions to each piece of media you encounter? What current practices will you change in response to this knowledge? How are you affected by manipulative information? How have they been effective in convincing you to believe in their content? What methods do you apply to verify the legitimacy of the content? How do you know the truth behind the content? Will you think differently regarding their information? How can you better prepare to handle more and more media outlets, as they are conforming to the freedom to deceive? Knowing their intent is to *control* you, how will you respond? Will you allow them to control you and connect the dots for you? Or will you take steps of awareness and program your mind to automatically *question the intent* of the content? It is important to arm yourself with the necessary information based on your decision. What research will you do to verify sources and content? Be careful and methodical as you analyze your research. It is helpful to understand how manipulation is used.

Keys to successful manipulation:

1. *Utilizing and controlling appropriate media outlets.* The government and other political venues have successfully gained control of nearly all major news and media outlets. This was not an accidental occurrence. And it was also not a sudden occurrence. When did you come to an awareness

that this was happening? Who owns the different outlets? What are the connections among the owners? What is the agenda of having a monopoly over major media sources? What are the possible outcomes of the monopoly? How could, or does, this affect you? What conclusion do you come to regarding this movement of control? What are the possible benefits of total control? What are the disadvantages of total control?

Who are they trying to manipulate? What seems to be the reason for the manipulation? What are the desired end results of doing this? How could this change things? How does *any* monopoly have positive outcomes? Who does the manipulation benefit? Does the source of the media outlets appear to have an agenda regarding the manipulation? Are they overlooking, ignoring, or leaving out information that doesn't support their agenda? Are they using unnecessary persuasive language to sway the audience's perception of a fact?

How will you research the content provided? How will you verify the validity of the information? Ensure you seek the most relevant information as you collect as much data as possible. Evaluate all of the raw data and extrapolate potential outcomes. Draw your own conclusion. Do you realize you are not as "free" as you once thought you were?

2. *Taking away the individual.* The government is trying desperately and is succeeding in manipulating people into forming groups and group mentality. They are "afraid" to have people think and act individually and be a strong force of their own, with their own thoughts, agenda, and individual actions. People can be very powerful when they use their own logic and intellect—so powerful, in fact, that they are feared. Thus, movements have been well underway to promote groups of people, encouraging them to pick an "identity" or, in some way, be a part of a group and engage in emotional bonds to keep their focus on that group rather than realizing *individual* rights are being absorbed by the government, thereby *weakening* the "people" as a whole.

They are *dividing* us. Being a part of a group is not a concern until it becomes focused on an *emotional* endeavor, giving more and more power to the *governing body* rather than to the rights of the *individual*. It is all a *loss of control* for the people and *more strength* for the government. Who is in charge of promoting "groupthink"? What seems to be the reason for this happening? What appears to be the desired end results of group thinking? How could this change things? Who does this benefit? Does the source of this information appear to have an underlying agenda? Is the agenda to help, nourish, encourage, and grow you? Is the source overlooking, ignoring, or leaving out information that doesn't support its agenda? Is the source using unnecessary persuasive language to sway your perception of a fact?

What research can be performed from a neutral and unbiased source to find out more information? What would the result be of weakening the unity of the people as a whole? How can we all still be our own individuals, yet stand *together* as *individuals* and *strengthen each other* as a country rather than *hand over control* to the government? What would the benefits be if we could all be ourselves as individuals and support each other, yet not give over our control to the government? What if we relinquished "group thinking" and used our own *individual* power and ability to think critically and analyze situations with the goal of a *stronger and unified* country?

3. *Developing fear in people.* Fear is the *primary* way to gain *control* over people. When people "feel" afraid or that they are in some way in harm, they bow down to authority quickly. Look how easy it was to create a worldwide stir and make people "want" to stay home and wear masks, even while alone in a desolate place. Fear is the only way to create a movement on such a large scale.

Can you think of any other way to make people *willingly* concede to having spiked protein factories

STUDENTS: WHO CONNECTS YOUR DOTS?

injected into them, and in some cases, two, three, four, and even five times? What research has been done to learn more about the source of the "virus"? How about the experimental "vaccine"? Have you found evidence proving the virus has actually been around for quite a while *prior* to the claim? What news outlet did you gather information about it from upon discovering it? Was the information you collected from a "major news outlet" which has permission and encouragement to *deceive?*

How effective were the volatile words *(urgent, critical, deadly, pandemic)* at achieving the desired effect—gaining *control* over people? Who is stirring up fear? How effective is fear in forcing people to do something? What seems to be the underlying reason for this happening? What appears to be the desired end result of the fear? How could this change things? Who does the fear benefit? Is there some sort of funding involved or a financial incentive? Does the source of this information appear to have an agenda? Is the source overlooking, ignoring, or leaving out information that doesn't support its agenda?

Has anyone been censored if they shared an opposing view? Is the source using unnecessary and persuasive language to sway the audience's perception of the facts? Was the media "fair and unbiased"? Where can you go to find scientific evidence? What information can morticians, embalmers, and funeral directors who have seen the resulting evidence of the claims, and in this case, the experimental "vaccine" provide?[15]

How can you undergo unbiased research and find answers for yourself? Search for as many resources as possible from both sides of the argument. Be sure to find credible sources to discover the most relevant information regarding this data and gather as much as possible. Use your own ability to infer and draw conclusions after evaluating all of the data.

4. *Creating a "solution."* Once fear is instilled, the next step is to create a solution. For instance, as popular computer software became available decades ago, computers and systems were running amazingly well. Perhaps too well. How could this be profitable? What could make it *more* profitable? How about a virus to create a purpose for purchasing more products to resolve the new issue? Thus, the invention of computer viruses and another lucrative endeavor.

   How about for a human-infected virus? Then, there would be a demand for a "vaccine" to counter the virus. Governing bodies have chosen this method of creating a problem and then creating a solution for generations. As it stands, it is extremely desirable to get any vaccine approved for the childhood list of vaccines. This is a goal of Big Pharma in order to secure *enormous* profits.[14] It then becomes a money factory.

   Who is creating a solution? Who is funding the research to make this possible? What seems to be the claim for the solution? What are the desired end results of the solution? How could this change things? Who does the solution benefit? Is there extensive research proving the safety of the solution? Where can you find credible data regarding the safety of the solution? Does the source of the solution appear to have an agenda? Is there a monetary benefit to the source of the solution? Are there any alternate solutions? Who else may benefit? Is there a secondary agenda? Is the source overlooking, ignoring, falsifying, or leaving out information that does not support its claim?

   Is there censorship for anyone with opposing views? Is the source of the solution using persuasive language to sway people's perception of the facts? What research can you perform using valid, detailed, and unbiased sources? Where can you find reliable and the most relevant information? Always, always, perform your own research, and choose credible and multiple sources. Evaluate all of the information collected and draw your own conclusions.

5. *Changing or creating laws to fit the agenda.* Just as occurred in 2013, a method of manipulation may be established by changing laws to fit an agenda. This could happen at any level, but people already in authority are generally the ones who have the power to do this. Sure enough, in 2013, the Act was signed to allow and encourage the media to deceive the American people through propaganda. When you can force people to be subjected to certain things, there is a greater chance that submission to the influence will occur.

What situation can you think of in which a law or rule was established or adjusted to fit someone else's specific agenda? Who changed the laws? What seems to be the reason for the changes? What are the desired end results of changing the law? How could this change things? Who received benefits from this occurrence? How are you affected by it?

Does the source of the changed laws appear to have an agenda? What does it appear to be? Is the source stacking hidden clauses buried deep within another law to ensure its passage? Is the source overlooking, ignoring, or leaving out pertinent information that does not support its claim? Is the source using unnecessarily persuasive language to sway the people's perception of facts?

How can you evaluate the situation so you understand the terms? What do you see if you look at things from the opposing perspective? How can you protect yourself from manipulation? How do you know when you are being controlled, deceived, or manipulated? Where can you find unbiased information? Gather as much data as possible from credible sources. Use your ability to infer to discover potential conclusions.

6. *Taking control of positions of power.* In order to influence a massive number of people, it is necessary to be in a

position of power or know someone in such a position. How can a position of power give an extra advantage? Who is the main target of interest for this position? What is the particular position? What seems to be the reason for the certain position? Is it a position of power? Who funded the campaign? What connection or involvement do they have? What or who does the position control? What appears to be the desired end result of being in the position? How could this change things?

Will they be working in your favor? Who else might they be working for? What does the position have authority over? Are the policies or rules created and enforced for the best interest of the people being served? Who benefits from them being in this position? Who benefits from their decisions? How does this affect you? What appears to be the agenda of being in this position? Does there appear to be any *hidden* agendas? How does "the source" benefit from being in this position? How can you find out the intent of the actions? Are there alternate people interested in this position? Who is the best qualified for this position?

Did the source resort to downplaying or humiliating their opponent in order to make themselves look better for the position? Is there any effort for deception in attaining this position? Does the source use persuasive language to sway the people's perception of the facts? What is the basis for their campaign or selection?

Do extensive research for every elected official promoting something questionable. Find sources of information regarding all people running for a position of power, including opposing sides. Put aside your biases and prejudices and gather information from multiple, credible, and varying resources. Collect as much information as possible. Determine which information is most relevant, evaluate and analyze all data, extrapolate and discover facts, and draw conclusions without prejudice or influence from anyone else.

7. *Developing a dependency in people.* Submission can be gained by developing a dependency within the people toward the ones in authority. This can be developed through numerous avenues, including fear, group thinking, deceit from the media, etc. Successful leadership involves the one in the position of authority, *serving* the needs of those who did the electing. Unfortunately, governing officials have somehow abused their power and turned the positions into self-serving agendas that involve manipulating the people to serve their needs and desires.

   Who is working for whom? Who is causing a dependency? Why might there be a need for the dependency? What seems to be the desired end result of the dependency? How could this change things? Who is the focus of the agenda? How can you become more independent?

   How does the government use the media to create a dependency within people? Who benefits from this dependency? How does this affect you? What happens if the majority of people become dependent on the government?

   How can you find relevant and unbiased information about this topic? Collect as much information as possible regarding dependency. Evaluate and analyze the information. Draw your own conclusions using your own unbiased logic.

8. *Creating controversy.* Did you happen to notice the real *enhanced* issue of racism, fascism, and other politically overutilized "-isms" only progressed when the first black president came into office and *promoted and exploited* this idea? Do your own research and gather facts regarding this topic. If you divide the country and the people, the government becomes *stronger,* and the people become *weaker.*

   So many groups have fallen for this tactic and played right into the hands of the instigators. There is now more reliance *by* the people *on* the government. This is *exactly* the intent of the effort. In this sense, the government is becoming *more* powerful. Who started the instigating? What might the motives be for this movement of creating *emotional-based* controversies? Who benefits from a stronger government and weaker people? What is the desired outcome of controversy among the people? How does the government become stronger as the people become weaker? What are the potential outcomes of this result?

How does this concern you? How do you fit into this scenario? What research can you do to find out facts for clarification? What sources can you identify that will provide unbiased information? What would happen if the government and media would stop promoting the idea of these "-isms"?

Collect as much data as possible. Develop an eye for unsourced claims, and consider why they are not forthcoming with the source. Where is censorship occurring? Draw your own independent conclusions from the raw data you collected. Have you noticed any of your freedoms slipping away?

9. *Destroying the family.* If there is a breakdown in the family, there is a *lack* of unity and strength in raising children under family terms. The children become elements of the court system and are immediately under *more control* of governing decisions. Each parent has a loss of rights in raising the child, and now the child is able to succumb more readily to the manipulation of others with an agenda, one of which is not in the child's best interest.

The public school system also has the freedom to manipulate children under governmental control, at the lowest of grade levels, and has had decades-plus of years to program them to their agenda. How could the influence of others program the minds of children? Who is trying to destroy the family unity? What seems to be the reasoning for this happening? What appears to be the desired end results of this? How could this change things? Who does destroying the family unit benefit? Does the source for this breakdown appear to have an agenda? Is the source overlooking, ignoring, or leaving out information that doesn't support its beliefs? Is the source using unnecessary language to sway the people's perception of the facts?

How could the breakdown of the family be detrimental for the "individual" versus the "government"? How could a strong family unit strengthen the unity within a country? How could a strong family unit weaken the government? What effects do you see with the breakdown of the family?

What type of unbiased research can be performed to find out more information? Find credible sources and gather as much information as possible. Research and then analyze all of the data collected. Formulate your own conclusions without prejudice.

10. *Destroying the churches.* Churches are a unit of strength with an image of morality or some sort of moral code. Each one may stand on its own ground and for possibly different things. Yet it is something that the government fears, as it threatens their agenda.

    What would be the result of weakening or breaking down the unity of churches? Who is attempting to do this? What appears to be the desired end result of the disunity of the church? How would this change things? Who would benefit from this? How would this change the moral code of governing bodies? Does the source of this destruction appear to have an agenda? Is the source overlooking, ignoring, or leaving out information that doesn't support its agenda? Is the source using unnecessary influence to sway the people's perception of the facts?

    Where can you research using unbiased resources? What do different churches stand for? Why might the government be threatened by them? Who benefits from the strength and teachings of a church? Using credible sources, perform extensive and thorough research regarding this topic. Ask lots of questions, and seek as much information as possible without prejudice. Evaluate, analyze, and draw your own independent conclusions.

11. *Taking over the educational system.* It is not an accident that government sources have taken over and monopolized *control* over the public school system and the *content* of information pushed onto the children and in universities. From the earliest stages of school life through college, and even in advanced education, the government has taken over control of education.

    By brainwashing vulnerable people willing to learn and absorb information presented from whom they believe to be trusted sources, the political agenda has been advancing for generations. How are students in most educational systems being brainwashed and manipulated with an intentional agenda? What seems to be the reason for this happening? What appears to be the desired end results? How will this change things? Who does this benefit? Why was God taken out of the public school system? Why are political agendas inserted into them?

    What is the premise of controlling the responses students give? How are students' opinions being controlled by the educational system? How might capturing the minds of children in the early years of education benefit the agenda of those who control the system? Is unnecessary language being used for purposes of persuasion? Who is funding large universities? Is information being left out or deceptive?

    How can you find unbiased research regarding this topic? What do you think is going on? Utilize the research gathered and formulate your own unbiased and independent conclusions.

It is vital to think critically about ways manipulation can and will occur. There is no doubt you are surrounded by propaganda and manipulation. Do your own independent and unbiased research and discover information from opposing sides. Formulate your own conclusions following adequate and thorough research. Find out where it takes you. Does any of it come as a surprise? What area has the greatest impact on you? Why do you think that is? What have you learned? How are you affected by this information?

Now that propaganda has been released like a "genie from a bottle," there is no "putting it back." How does the propaganda in social media affect you? Families? Businesses? Other groups or organizations? How about Big Pharma and their new era of explicitly and carelessly promoting drugs and their agenda on all media sources now? Are you concerned with this advertising and subliminal messages, knowing the permission to deceive? How can you protect yourself from false or altered truth information? Who benefits from this information? There are so many questions to be asked and information to be verified. Be careful as you navigate the muddy (and often polluted) waters of propaganda, and remember to think critically and perform extensive independent research before formulating conclusions.

The most effective way to destroy people is to deny and obliterate their own understanding of their history.
—George Orwell

Propaganda is to a democracy what the bludgeon is to a totalitarian state.
—Noam Chomsky

You can sway a thousand men by appealing to their prejudices quicker than you can convince one man by logic.
—Robert A. Heinlein

The whole aim of practical politics is to keep the population alarmed (and hence clamorous

to be led to safety) by an endless series of hobgoblins, most of them imaginary.
—H.L. Mencken

Modern industrial civilization has developed within a certain system of convenient myths. The driving force of modern industrial civilization has been individual material gain, which is accepted as legitimate, even praiseworthy, on the grounds that private vices yield public benefits in the classic formulation. Now, it's long been understood very well that a society that is based on this principle will destroy itself in time. It can only persist with whatever suffering and injustice it entails as long as it's possible to pretend that the destructive forces that humans create are limited: that the world is an infinite garbage can. At this stage of history, either one of two things is possible: either the general population will take control of its own destiny and will concern itself with community interests, guided by values of solidarity and sympathy and concern for others, or, alternatively, there will be no destiny for anyone to control. As long as some specialized class is in a position of authority, it is going to set policy for the special interests that it serves. But the conditions of survival, let alone justice, require rational social planning in the interests of the community as a whole, and, by now, that means the global community. The question is whether privileged elites should dominate mass communication and should use this power as they tell us they must, namely, to impose necessary illusions, manipulate and deceive the stupid majority, and remove them from the public arena. The question, in brief, is whether democracy and freedom are values to be preserved or threats to be avoided. In this possibly terminal phase of human existence, democracy, and freedom are more than values to be treasured; they may well be essential to survival.
—Noam Chomsky

STUDENTS: WHO CONNECTS YOUR DOTS?

 Reflect:

1. How have you noticed changes in propaganda through the past five years? Ten?
2. How does propaganda affect you? Your family? Your community?
3. How could propaganda be used to the benefit of the American people? How about to the detriment of them?
4. What is your biggest concern regarding the current status of propaganda in all of the major media sources, Big Pharma, Big Tech, etc.?
5. Have you ever allowed yourself to be influenced and swayed by media manipulation? Name a topic that drew you in emotionally to their persuasion. What did you do right? What changes would you make to your response? How does your opinion differ due to this presented information?
6. How will you evaluate or research information that you feel is concerning? How will you verify the credibility of your resources?
7. What other forms of manipulation can you add to the list included in this chapter? How would you think critically about the additional forms you came up with?
8. Read the books, references, or even the cliff notes or a summary, plus the Act mentioned in this chapter. How do you see a correlation to where we are today? What other titles can you think of that have the same source of information regarding this topic?
9. What other thoughts do you have regarding propaganda?

CHAPTER 21

Why Censor?

"Censorship is the suppression of speech, public communication, or other information."[16]

"Political censorship exists when a government attempts to conceal, fake, distort, or falsify information that its citizens receive by suppressing or crowding out political news that the public might receive through news outlets."[16]

People are unable to dissent from the government or political party in charge in the absence of neutral or objective information. This is something they count on.

"This term also extends to the systematic suppression of views that are contrary to those of the government in power. The government often possesses the power of the army and the secret police to enforce the compliance of journalists with the will of the authorities to spread the story that the ruling authorities want the people to believe. At times, this involves bribery, defamation, imprisonment, and even assassination."[16]

There are many different forms of censorship found in many different arenas. There is even self-censorship, sometimes used by authors, artists, inventors, etc., to protect their artistic work. It is important not only to be aware that censorship exists but also to be able to think critically through each case of censorship you may encounter. You need to be able to draw your own conclusions based on logic and sound reasoning backed by evidence and raw data. Lacking the ability to think critically could be detrimental to your ability to come to a truth-based conclusion. You must possess the ability to analyze information effectively and without prejudice.

Your "freedoms" in society today are disappearing faster than at any other time in history. There is a risk at hand if you do not learn to think more critically. There is a greater chance that you will succumb to fraud, manipulation, gaslighting, propaganda, etc., if you cannot think critically. Is there any evidence of censorship that you see in society today? Analyze the issue of censorship and all facts, data, and evidence related to it. The challenge is to do so without the influence of personal feelings, opinions, or biases. Analyze based on factual information only.

Once again, go back to the Act passed in 2013, permitting and encouraging false, deceptive, and mis- or disinformation in propaganda. As mentioned earlier, having read or listened to this, you now know that the censorship by the major news and social media outlets is not due to any form of misinformation since this was approved in 2013. Simply put, censorship is fear. Fear that others will find out. Therefore, what are they afraid of? What don't they want you to know? The truth? Why are they censoring some of the most intelligent and talented people in the world for speaking out about what they personally witnessed in their fields of expertise? Any form of censorship, other than personal censorship to protect your own artistic work, should raise a flag of alert and make you desire to seek additional information, which includes extensive research regarding opposing views of the topic at hand. Censorship is based on an *insecurity* of the one doing the censoring. It is a fear of someone revealing something that the "censor" doesn't want others to know. This should always make you begin the process of CT.

Who is doing the censoring? What seems to be the reason for the censoring? What appears to be the desired end result? How could this change things? Who does the censoring benefit? Does the source of censoring appear to have an agenda? Is it emotionally driven? Is the source of the censoring overlooking, ignoring, or leaving out information that doesn't support its beliefs or claims? Is the source of the censoring using unnecessary language to sway an audience's perception of a fact?

Remember, your ability to independently research is a key to having authenticity. Verify your sources of information and evaluate them within your own means. If sources you discover are not willing to expose where the information came from, let that be a red flag to you. Verify your sources. If possible, evaluate claims from both sides of an argument, being aware of possible biases from either or both sides. Practice setting aside your own personal biases, as this will most likely cloud your judgment. Learn to see things from alternate vantage points.

Do you identify censorship in the news media outlets today? How about social media? How about in the entertainment industry? What about in the government or politics in general? How about on a local level, within your community? Where else do you see censorship occurring? Have you ever censored anyone from anything? Has anyone ever censored you personally? Think critically about the reasons behind each of the scenarios mentioned. Ask objective and unbiased questions. Always select the most important and relevant information regarding the topic; in this case, censorship.

Determine what establishes clear direction in what you are trying to figure out. What is your end goal? Once you have gathered and collected the most relevant material, assess the information and draw your own conclusions based on the unbiased data. This is such an important skill in mastering the art of CT.

What have you concluded about censorship? How do you see it in your surrounding environment? Be aware of the occurrences, and think critically in each case.

Censorship is to art, as lynching is to justice.
—Henry Louis Gates Jr

STUDENTS: WHO CONNECTS YOUR DOTS?

Whoever would overthrow the liberty of a nation must begin by subduing the freeness of speech.
—Benjamin Franklin

Let us be clear: censorship is cowardice. It masks corruption. It is a school of torture: it teaches and accustoms one to the use of force against an idea, to submit thought to an alien "other." But worst still, censorship destroys criticism, which is the essential ingredient of culture.
—Pablo Antonio Cuadra

Once a government is committed to the principle of silencing the voice of opposition, it has only one way to go, and that is down the path of increasingly repressive measures until it becomes a source of terror to all its citizens and creates a country where everyone lives in fear.
—Henry S. Truman

Think for yourselves and let others enjoy the privilege to do so, too.
—Voltaire

 Reflect:

1. Where do you notice censorship in the world today? Is there any currently affecting you?
2. Summarize the key elements of the censorship. What conclusions do you draw?
3. How does the idea of censorship compare and contrast to the culture you live in today?

4. What sources did you use to evaluate the censorship? What information did you see as most relevant? What are the *real* reasons for censorship?
5. What is your biggest concern regarding the conclusions you came to regarding censorship? What is the premise of your concern?
6. How will you use this information in your daily life? How does it affect you?

CHAPTER 22

Why Cancel?

> *"Cancel culture, also known as call-out culture, is a phrase contemporary to the late two thousand tens to two thousand twenties used to refer to a culture in which those who are deemed to have acted or spoken in an unacceptable manner are ostracized, boycotted, or shunned. This shunning may extend to social or professional circles—whether on social media or in person—with most high-profile incidents involving celebrities. Those subject to this ostracism are said to have been "canceled.""*[17]

"Canceling" can also be in the form of publicly shaming a person or group of people. It could also mean withdrawing support for some form of public figure or company based on something they did or said that was found to be in some way "offensive" or objectionable. It is a form of rejection that potentially denies someone the right to apologize or somehow resolve a mistake that may have been made. Whether a mistake or simply being objectionable, the possibility of being "called out" exists within the terms of the "cancel culture."

"Canceling" also stems from issues of insecurity and a deep-seated need for control. It is a version of "stomping your feet" to get your way and denying someone the right to their opinion or freedom of speech. Apply the same measures of CT to the issues involving "cancel culture." What is the source of information? Where did it come from? Was it independently verified? How do you evaluate the source of information? How about the content of the information? What is the reliability of the source and the content? Do you fully understand the information collected? What additional resources have been used for interpretation?

What is the premise of the argument for canceling? Who stands to benefit from it? Who is doing what regarding canceling? What seems to be the goal, or end result, of the canceling? How could this change things? What was the position of the one being canceled? What appeared to be the premise? Evaluate the claims on both sides of the argument. View things from differing points of view. Does the source of canceling appear to have an agenda? Is it overlooking or intentionally leaving out information that opposes its claim? Is it using unnecessary language to sway the audience to its cancellation?

Assess the information regarding the canceling issue independently, extrapolating and discovering potential outcomes. Make a conscious effort to remain unbiased and use only relevant information based on confirmed and trusted sources. Using logical reasoning based on factual information, what do you think is going on?

How is "canceling" linked to conformity? Is it yet another method to snatch away your freedom? How do you perceive it in relation to a form of control? Realize the ones who do the canceling are the ones who are afraid, insecure, and trying to bully their way to power and control. They do not want you to think for yourself and, especially, express your own opinion if it differs from theirs. Understanding the source and the reasoning allows you to see more clearly when this is happening, by whom, and why.

Continue to utilize the same methods of CT presented in this book. Train yourself to analyze situations using relevant, factual, and unbiased sources, looking at them from opposing perspectives. Is the process of CT becoming easier? Have you noticed yourself asking the same form of questions almost instinctively? Take the time to program this information into your mind so you become automatically programmed to think critically and instinctively regarding all matters.

STUDENTS: WHO CONNECTS YOUR DOTS?

In a cancel culture, we appoint ourselves the arbiters of right and wrong and also the judge and jury because, thanks to social media, we get to dole out punishment.
—Unknown

Cancel culture is not actually about justice. It is about control. People use cancellation to force conformity to ideals.
—Teal Swan

Cancel culture is a pretentious form of bullying.
—Unknown

Cancel culture is a term bounced around by people afraid of accountability. But freedom of speech does not mean freedom from consequences.
—Monisha Rajesh

Cancel culture grows because we accept (and gluttonously consume) social violence. We no longer seek truth or both sides of a story. Whichever side is loudest wins…regardless of its relationship to the truth.
—Steve Maraboli

We live in a generation of emotionally weak people. Everything has to be watered down because it's offensive, including the truth.
—Unknown

 Reflect:

1. Where do you notice cancel culture in the world today? How does it affect you?
2. Summarize the key elements of the cancel culture. What information do you draw from this?

3. How does the idea of cancel culture compare and contrast to the culture you live in today?
4. What sources did you use to evaluate the cancel culture? What information do you see as most relevant?
5. What is your biggest concern regarding your conclusions about cancel culture today? What is the premise of your concern?
6. Are you personally affected by a "cancel"? If so, explain.

CHAPTER 23

Conclusion

After much discussion and review of various ideas, thoughts, stories, and concepts, what have you concluded regarding *Students: Who Connects Your Dots?* Did you determine whether or not other news media sources have taken on this role and taken over the connection for you? What about the internet or other students or peers? Social media? Or did you determine that *you* actually are in control of CT and connecting your own dots by utilizing your own sound analysis and evaluation? Are there any changes or alterations you need or would like to make? Where will you be applying CT methods? Who else could benefit from gaining an understanding of this process?

How about regarding decision-making? Who connects your decision-making dots? Are you easily persuaded by a news source you overheard or a friend you admire? Or do you consider what you hear and evaluate the information based on facts and logic? Have you gained an understanding of the importance of thinking critically by your own means?

It is both fascinating and concerning to think about how many sources and which ones have programmed your mind since the day you were born. If not addressed, these other influences could continue to be the reason you respond as you do, sometimes challenging your very own values. Has the presented information caused you to think about the current programming of your mind? In the book *Elevate Your Mind to Success,* the foundation is laid for the basis of the preprogrammed mind and provides detailed thoughts, ideas, and suggestions on how to acknowledge your current programming, then remove, replace, and reframe your unwanted thoughts to align with your current design of values and beliefs. This ties in with the focused and pragmatic ability to think critically, especially regarding sensitive or controversial matters. You must know who you are and what you believe in to properly reprogram your mind to instinctively and positively respond in ways that supportively align with your values.

Be "on the lookout" for bias in the world that surrounds you. You will find that it is everywhere you look. It is tempting to succumb to the strategically "offensive" biases and respond with a just-as-emotional "defensive" reply. However, this could only further escalate the topic or situation at hand, flaring additional emotions in a senseless tizzy, all while defying logical thought. Take a step back, or maybe even two, and engage your powerfully effective CT skills in an unbiased effort to draw on verified, extrapolated, and factual data, leading to logical insight.

In previous chapters, you learned how to discover unbiased yet factual research material and methods and do your own analysis and evaluation. Use your CT skills to evaluate opposing sides to bring more enlightenment to your analysis. Awareness is always the first step in any situation. Start to understand what and why things are progressing the way they are. And the key here is to ascertain this information independently and free from prejudice.

Students: Who Connects Your Dots? defines the vital CT method regarding both decision-making and evaluating the truthfulness of information, the basis for the need to think critically, and how to perform it properly. It is imperative to bring yourself to a complete understanding of the methods and particulars of thinking in this manner. CT is a skill that must be practiced and mastered in order to contend with this vastly changing culture. Taking an unbiased stance is necessary for the ability to comprehend all aspects of a situation and develop insight from all perspectives. Just as with the success of the Trojan horse in the city of Troy, there is always more clarity and a better position when you have access to the opposing side's most vulnerable information. It is also imperative that you collect as much data as possible before reaching an informed and logical decision.

STUDENTS: WHO CONNECTS YOUR DOTS?

In addition, as more knowledge is gained, more doors may open with possibilities of an altered opinion or way of doing things. Always be open to the possibility of absorbing new information, which may lead to a fresh perspective you may have been previously unaware of. You may discover missing pieces to a story that change your entire perspective. If you are not open to the possibility, you may be supporting something unintentional or unfavorable to your true beliefs.

In early chapters, there were discussions regarding handling emotionally presented information and methods of making logical decisions despite the potential challenge. Often, people tend to "cave in" when someone approaches with an aggressive demeanor. *Students: Who Connects Your Dots?* gave ideas on identifying, preparing for, and handling situations such as this.

Healthy relationships are important to everyone. This is essential to a healthy, happy, and joy-filled lifestyle. The importance of healthy relationships was highlighted as many different forms were presented, along with the benefits and process of nurturing them. Relationships are most important and deserve extra time, consideration, compassion, and empathy. *Students* looked at the intricacies involved in various types of relationships, including the importance of the innate spiritual connection with your Creator, as well as peer pressure situations and how to apply CT to each one. Along with relationships, correctly chosen activities are important to a fulfilling livelihood, and a look at how to make good choices in activities, as well as academic importance, was addressed.

The Milgram Experiment, performed by Stanley Milgram, was brought forth and discussed, revealing human behavior regarding obedience while under authority. From these experiments, we learned that ordinary people might likely follow orders from an authority figure for one of many reasons, even to the extent of killing innocent human beings. Obedience to authority is ingrained in people to the degree it has been preprogrammed into their minds. People are capable of acting as agents for another person's will. Along with the guise of authority, many other factors are influential in "persuading" decision-making in people, which were discussed in previous chapters. Be aware of these factors and how people can be easily influenced by others to do unethical or even unexplainable things while under their misguided pretenses.

Social media and electronics are a constant part of the current lifestyle and taking over a greater role daily. It is, therefore, essential to think critically about how they are utilized. CT methods were implored and practiced on a series of thought-provoking topics, including for potential reasons of feeling a need to identify and the common and growing stance today of placing blame on others rather than taking responsibility or being accountable for actions of self. Both of these topics appeared to have "grown wings" of their own and have "taken flight." A source of this focus has been through numerous sources of propaganda. Propaganda was defined, along with its intention to control how you think and act. Propaganda relies on manipulation, and keys to successful manipulation were explored and discussed for thinking application. Discussion ensued regarding the book *Nineteen Eighty-Four* to exemplify the ingenious "premonition" of George Orwell regarding the potential result of manipulation, control, and brainwashing of people by authority figures with a self-serving agenda.

Students also described the importance of building up character qualities such as kindness, compassion, resilience, perseverance, and determination as proponents of essential leadership skills and qualities important for future careers. Refined communication is always a necessity, and *Students* even described steps to becoming positively captivating.

CT was also applied to finances, and processes were outlined to manage money efficiently and effectively. Budgeting is a crucial method of planning what to do with your money. It is an important way to become debt-free *and* create a healthy savings account. Processes were described, showing steps on how to get started and maintain a debt-free life.

And finally, censorship and cancel culture were defined and processed through the CT method. CT is more important and vital than ever before. Being skillfully adept at this process helps awaken and potentially "immunize" you to the negative effects of manipulation, persuasion, and influence of powerful governing bodies that surround

STUDENTS: WHO CONNECTS YOUR DOTS?

you, at least to a certain extent. It takes dedication, hard work, and a concentrated effort to master CT skills. *Students: Who Connects Your Dots* has broken down the basic elements of CT and has offered ideas, suggestions, examples, and questions to hone your skills in order to become a better, and even instinctual, critical thinker. By performing these skills, you will use logic to make informed, factual, and unbiased decisions, giving you an edge on your individuality and strength in your freedom against conformity.

The third-rate mind is only happy when it is thinking with the majority. A second-rate mind is only happy when it is thinking with the minority. A first-rate mind is only happy when it is thinking.
—A.A. Milne

The important thing is not to stop questioning. Curiosity has its own reason for existing.
—Albert Einstein

It is a mark of an educated mind to be able to entertain a thought without accepting it.
—Aristotle

Critical thinking is not something you do once with an issue and then drop it. It requires that we update our knowledge as new information comes in.
—Daniel Levitin

The essence of the independent mind lies not in what it thinks but in how it thinks.
—Christopher Hitchens

Freethinkers are those who are willing to use their minds without prejudice and without fearing to understand things that clash with their own customs,

privileges, or beliefs. This state of mind is not common, but it is essential for critical thinking.
—Leo Tolstoy

To think incisively and to think for one's self is very difficult. We are prone to let our mental life become invaded by legions of half-truths, prejudices, and propaganda. At this point, I wonder whether or not education is fulfilling its purpose. A great majority of the so-called educated people do not think logically and scientifically. Even the press, the classroom, the platforms, and the pulpit, in many instances, do not give us objective and unbiased truths. To save man from the morass of propaganda, in my opinion, is one of the chief aims of education. Education must enable one to sift and weigh evidence, to discern the true from the false, the real from the unreal, and the facts from the fiction. The function of education, therefore, is to teach one to think intensively and to think critically.
—Dr. Martin Luther King, Jr

 Reflect:

1. Define the skill of CT. Summarize the key elements of it. How will you apply these particular skills in your daily life?
2. How will you word questions so they are framed in an unbiased stance? Make a list of questions you will ask yourself when you employ the CT process.
3. What sources will you use to educate yourself further on CT? How will you choose the sources? How will you validate the integrity of the sources?
4. Who did you discover connects your dots? Are there any changes you will make based on this discovery?

STUDENTS: WHO CONNECTS YOUR DOTS?

5. How do you handle a "hyped" person? How did you develop the skills to be successful at this?
6. Are all of your relationships healthy? What changes do you need to make?
7. How can you extend more kindness to others? What are you already doing correctly?
8. How well do you maintain your health? Are there any changes you need to make?
9. How well do you communicate? What are you doing well? What areas could use some improvement? How will you pursue this?
10. Where do you volunteer your time or services?
11. Describe your leadership skills. How will you continue to add to your skills?
12. How well do you manage your finances? Do you need to make any changes? What budget tool do you use?
13. What are your thoughts about propaganda? What is your biggest insight or concern about the conclusions you came to regarding the manipulation surrounding you? What is the premise of your concern?
14. How has this information impacted the way you think?
15. How will you apply the information you learned from this book to your daily life?
16. Who will you share this information with?

Critical Thinking Questions

*To discover the truth, you must first
ask the right questions.*
—Jill Fandrich

Decision-Making Questions:

Who will be affected by your decision?
How will you or they be affected by your decision?
Will anyone get hurt in the process?
Will your decision be something you can be proud of?
How will the decision shape your reputation or future?
How will the decision grow you as a person?
What is the right thing to do?
What obstacles might be clouding your judgment?
What option will lead to the best possible outcome?
What decision will be best for your legacy?

Evaluating Information From a Situation or Event:

Who is doing what?
What seems to be the reason for this happening?
What appears to be the desired end results?
How could they change?
What are the surrounding circumstances?
Whom does this benefit?
How does this affect you?
Does the source of this information appear to have an agenda?
What is the agenda?

STUDENTS: WHO CONNECTS YOUR DOTS?

Does the message have a bias?
Is the source overlooking, ignoring, or leaving out information that doesn't support its beliefs or claims?
Is there censoring involved for opposing views?
If so, why would this be?
Is the source using unnecessary or persuasive language to sway an audience's perception of a fact?
Is their funding involved?
Who is funding the source?
Is there a financial incentive involved?
How could this affect decisions?
How can you find reliable and credible resources?
How can you verify their credibility?
Is the information sourced or unsourced?
Is anything else being hidden?
What information is most relevant?
What other critical thoughts come to mind?
What do you think is going on?

Create Your Own Questions:

1.

2.

3.

4.

5.

Journal

Great thinkers are note-*worthy.*
—Jill Fandrich

Date:
Topic:

How could I have applied critical thinking to my interactions today?

What mistakes did I make?

How can I do it differently next time?

What did I do right?

What have I learned from this experience?

Other questions:

Journal

Great thinkers are note-*worthy.*
—Jill Fandrich

Date:
Topic:

How could I have applied critical thinking to my interactions today?

What mistakes did I make?

How can I do it differently next time?

What did I do right?

What have I learned from this experience?

Other questions:

Journal

Great thinkers are note-*worthy.*
—Jill Fandrich

Date:
Topic:

How could I have applied critical thinking to my interactions today?

What mistakes did I make?

How can I do it differently next time?

What did I do right?

What have I learned from this experience?

Other questions:

Journal

Great thinkers are note-*worthy.*
—Jill Fandrich

Date:
Topic:

How could I have applied critical thinking to my interactions today?

What mistakes did I make?

How can I do it differently next time?

What did I do right?

What have I learned from this experience?

Other questions:

Journal

Great thinkers are note-*worthy.*
—Jill Fandrich

Date:
Topic:

How could I have applied critical thinking to my interactions today?

What mistakes did I make?

How can I do it differently next time?

What did I do right?

What have I learned from this experience?

Other questions:

Journal

Great thinkers are note-*worthy.*
—Jill Fandrich

Date:
Topic:

How could I have applied critical thinking to my interactions today?

What mistakes did I make?

How can I do it differently next time?

What did I do right?

What have I learned from this experience?

Other questions:

Journal

Great thinkers are note-*worthy.*
—Jill Fandrich

Date:
Topic:

How could I have applied critical thinking to my interactions today?

What mistakes did I make?

How can I do it differently next time?

What did I do right?

What have I learned from this experience?

Other questions:

References

1. 6 Critical Thinking Skills You Need to Master Now, by Will Erstad; 1/22/2018; Accessed January 24, 2023; https://www.rasmussen.edu/student-experience/college-life/critical-thinking-skills-to-master-now/
2. Milgram Experiment; Wikipedia; Accessed January 28, 2023; https://en.m.wikipedia.org/wiki/Milgram_experiment
3. The Golden Ratio—The Creator's Mark Throughout His Creation, November 13, 2015, Christian Perspective, https://www.christianperspective.net/blog/the-golden-ratio-the-creators-mark-throughout-his-creation
4. God's Fingerprint – The Fibonacci Sequence, Accessed December 18, 2023, https://www.youtube.com/watch?v=Xw0iF0UstI0
5. What is the Fibonacci sequence?, by Tia Ghose, March 1, 2023, https://www.livescience.com/37470-fibonacci-sequence.html
6. What is Irreducible Complexity? By Discovery Science, https://www.youtube.com/watch?v=0cN-aIXNQrc
7. Revolutionary, by The Discovery Institute and Michael Behe, www.RevolutionaryBehe.com, https://revolutionarybehe.com
8. Is Genesis History? By Del Tackett, DM, Accessed December 17, 2023, https://www.youtube.com/watch?v=UM82qxxskZE
9. Financial Peace University, Ramseysolutions.com, accessed 12-17-2023, https://www.ramseysolutions.com/

ramseyplus/financial-peace?gad_source=1&gclid=CjwKC AiA1fqrBhA1EiwAMU5m_0ik_6nkd0foAVH7vOlMYjs 18qrwtczWxkIGK9ZC3wV_mA2pzrMbVxoCsYoQAvD _BwE

10. Propaganda by Edward Bernays; 2005; Ig Publishing; 168 pages.
11. U.S. Repeals Propaganda Ban, Spreads Government-Made News to Americans; By John Hudson. July 14, 2013; foreignpolicy.com; Accessed March 15, 2023; https://foreignpolicy.com/2013/07/14/u-s-repeals-propaganda-ban-spreads-government-made-news-to-Americans/
12. When Was 1984 Written?; Study.com; Liz Breazeale and Jenna Clayton; 12/02/2021; Accessed February 2, 2023; https://study.com/academy/lesson/when-was-1984-written.html
13. Turtles All The Way Down; Vaccine Science and Myth; all references; https://tinyurl.com/TurtlesBookEngRef
14. Turtles All The Way Down; free chapter 1; https://tinyurl.com/TurtlesBookChap1Eng
15. Died Suddenly 2022 (Full Documentary); Accesses March 15, 2023; https://rumble.com/v1wcs7o-died-suddenly-2022-full-documentary.html
16. Censorship; Wikipedia; 2023; Accessed January 30, 2023; https://en.m.wikipedia.org/wiki/Censorship
17. Cancel Culture; Wikipedia; 2023; Accesses January 3-, 2023; https://en.m.wikipedis.org/wiki/Cancel_culture